3/09

D1529951

The Boxer

OUR BEST FRIENDS

The Boxer
Caring for Your Mutt
The German Shepherd
The Golden Retriever
The Labrador Retriever
The Poodle
The Shih Tzu
The Yorkshire Terrier

OUR BEST FRIENDS

The Boxer

Chad Hautmann

ELDORADO INK

Produced by OTTN Publishing, Stockton, New Jersey

Eldorado Ink
PO Box 100097
Pittsburgh, PA 15233
www.eldoradoink.com

First printing

1 3 5 7 9 8 6 4 2

Library of Congress Cataloging-in-Publication Data

   Hautmann, Chad.
   The Boxer / Chad Hautmann.
      p. cm. — (Our best friends)
   Includes bibliographical references and index.
   ISBN-13: 978-1-932904-19-2 ((hc))
   ISBN-10: 1-932904-19-0 ((hc))
   1. Boxer (Dog breed) I. Title.
   SF429.B75H38 2008
   636.73—dc22

                  2007044874

Photo credits: © American Animal Hospital Association: 45; © iStockphoto.com/Justin Horrocks: 30, front cover (left center); © iStockphoto.com/Brad Johnson: 8, front cover (left bottom); © iStockphoto.com/Bruce Jolley: 42; © iStockphoto.com/Denisa Moorehouse: 88; © iStockphoto.com/Guillermo Perales: 99; © iStockphoto.com/Ludovic Rhodes: 89; © iStockphoto.com/Daniel Rodriguez: 101, back cover; © iStockphoto.com/walik: 32, 46, 50; Library of Congress: 20; Photos.com: 60; used under license from Shutterstock, Inc.: 3, 11, 12, 15, 17, 18, 22, 24, 27, 28, 34, 35, 37, 47, 48, 51, 52, 56, 57, 59, 63, 64, 66, 67, 68, 70, 71, 72, 75, 76, 77, 79, 82, 83, 85, 87, 92, 96, 97, front cover (main and left top).

TABLE OF CONTENTS

Introduction by Gary Korsgaard, DVM   6

1   Is a Boxer Your Kind of Dog?   9

2   History of the Boxer Breed   17

3   Being a Responsible Pet Owner   24

4   The Best Start for You and Your Dog   34

5   Caring for Your Puppy (Birth to Six Months)   52

6   Your "Teenage" Boxer (Six Months to Two Years)   70

7   Caring for Your Adult Boxer   82

8   The Later Years and Saying Good-bye   96

Organizations to Contact   102
Further Reading   105
Internet Resources   106
Index   108
Contributors   112

Introduction

GARY KORSGAARD, DVM

The mutually beneficial relationship between humans and animals began long before the dawn of recorded history. Archaeologists believe that humans began to capture and tame wild goats, sheep, and pigs more than 9,000 years ago. These animals were then bred for specific purposes, such as providing humans with a reliable source of food or providing furs and hides that could be used for clothing or the construction of dwellings.

Other animals had been sought for companionship and assistance even earlier. The dog, believed to be the first animal domesticated, began living and working with Stone Age humans in Europe more than 14,000 years ago. Some archaeologists believe that wild dogs and humans were drawn together because both hunted the same prey. By taming and training dogs, humans became more effective hunters. Dogs, meanwhile, enjoyed the social contact with humans and benefited from greater access to food and warm shelter. Dogs soon became beloved pets as well as trusted workers. This can be seen from the many artifacts depicting dogs that have been found at ancient sites in Asia, Europe, North America, and the Middle East.

The earliest domestic cats appeared in the Middle East about 5,000 years ago. Small wild cats were probably first attracted to human settlements because plenty of rodents could be found wherever harvested grain was stored. Cats played a useful role in hunting and killing these pests, and it is likely that grateful humans rewarded them for this assistance. Over time, these small cats gave up some of their aggressive wild behaviors and began living among humans. Cats eventually became so popular in ancient Egypt that they were believed to possess magical powers. Cat statues were placed outside homes to ward off evil spirits, and mummified cats were included in royal tombs to accompany their owners into the afterlife.

Today, few people believe that cats have supernatural powers, but most pet owners feel a magical bond with their pets, whether they are dogs, cats, hamsters, rabbits, horses, or parrots. The lives of pets and their people become inextricably intertwined, providing strong emotional and physical rewards for both humans and animals. People of all ages can benefit from the loving companionship of a pet. Not surprisingly, then, pet ownership is widespread. Recent statistics indicate that about 60 percent of all households in the United States and Canada have at least one pet, while the figure is close to 50 percent of households in the United Kingdom. For millions of people, therefore, pets truly have become their "best friends."

Finding the best animal friend can be a challenge, however. Not only are there many types of domesticated pets, but each has specific needs, characteristics, and personality traits. Even within a category of pets, such as dogs, different breeds will flourish in different surroundings and with different treatment. For example, a German Shepherd may not be the right pet for a person living in a cramped urban apartment; that person might be better off caring for a smaller dog like a Toy Poodle or Shih Tzu, or perhaps a cat. On the other hand, an active person who loves the outdoors may prefer the companionship of a Labrador Retriever to that of a small dog or a passive indoor pet like a goldfish or hamster.

The joys of pet ownership come with certain responsibilities. Bringing a pet into your home and your neighborhood obligates you to care for and train the pet properly. For example, a dog must be housebroken, taught to obey your commands, and trained to behave appropriately when she encounters other people or animals. Owners must also be mindful of their pet's particular nutritional and medical needs.

The purpose of the OUR BEST FRIENDS series is to provide a helpful and comprehensive introduction to pet ownership. Each book contains the basic information a prospective pet owner needs in order to choose the right pet for his or her situation and to care for that pet throughout the pet's lifetime. Training, socialization, proper nutrition, potential medical issues, and the legal responsibilities of pet ownership are thoroughly explained and discussed, and an abundance of expert tips and suggestions are offered. Whether it is a hamster, corn snake, guinea pig, or Labrador Retriever, the books in the OUR BEST FRIENDS series provide everything the reader needs to know about how to have a happy, well-adjusted, and well-behaved pet.

The muscular and athletic Boxer is among the most popular of dog breeds. Boxers make great pets because of their fierce loyalty, their high energy, and their sense of fun.

CHAPTER ONE

Is a Boxer Your Kind of Dog?

When you decide to share your life with a dog, you're doing far more than just acquiring a pet. Getting a dog is an investment in the future. In exchange for proper food, good care, exercise, a warm place to sleep, and lots of attention, your dog will give you a lifetime of undivided loyalty, joy, and love. That's a very good deal for both you and the dog.

There are innumerable dog breeds from which to choose. Because you have picked up this book, you must be considering a Boxer. That would be an outstanding choice, because the Boxer is an excellent dog.

Boxers are a hearty breed, square of form, solidly muscled, and short-haired. In fact, you could compare their appearance to the look of a well-chiseled pugilist, a middleweight, maybe, though that's not how the Boxer derived its name. The Boxer's color is generally either fawn or brindle (brindle is a gray or tan with stripes or spots of a slightly darker color).

What most people notice first about Boxers is their smart, alert look. Intelligence and curiosity are hallmarks of the breed. This curiosity, however, can be both a blessing and a challenge for the Boxer owner, because if a Boxer is not regularly stimulated mentally—by learning new tricks, seeing new places, or playing new games—she can unleash her inquisitiveness in less desirable ways around the house. For example, she may decide to see just how far a toilet paper roll will unravel or how many little scraps she can make of the Sunday paper. This holds true for the adult Boxer as well as the Boxer puppy. But most Boxer owners would agree that the breed's lifelong curiosity is one of its most endearing features.

BREED STANDARDS AND CONFORMATION

Each breed of purebred dog has a parent club, which is organized and led by experienced breeders and other fanciers of that breed. Each parent club develops a written description of the perfect dog of that breed, and this is the criterion by which dogs of that breed are judged in the show ring. This description is known as the Standard of Perfection, or the breed standard. The Standard of Perfection always covers the proper appearance and gait of pure-bred dogs, and many standards also include a description of the ideal temperament for the breed. Reputable breeders strive to produce dogs that conform to the Standard of Perfection as closely as possible.

The American Kennel Club, which is the largest organization that registers purebred dogs in the United States, posts the official breed standard developed by the American Boxer Club on its Web site, www.akc.org. The breed standard describes the Boxer as a "medium-sized, square-built dog of good substance with short back, strong limbs, and short, tight-fitting coat." The standard also notes that the Boxer was "developed to serve as [a] guard, working, and companion dog," and that the ideal Boxer "combines strength and agility with elegance and style." The breed standards formulated by Boxer clubs in Canada and the United Kingdom are very similar to the U.S. standard.

Boxers that don't match the breed standard can still make wonderful pets and companions. However, if you plan to enter your canine friend in dog shows, he'll need to match the AKC specifications as closely as possible. Dogs that don't conform to the breed standard will be disqualified from AKC-sanctioned Conformation shows. In

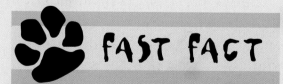

FAST FACT

Boxers love to work and are often employed as therapy dogs in hospitals, as search-and-rescue dogs, and as guide dogs for the visually impaired.

The breed standard establishes the ideal physical characteristics for Boxers, such as their size, proper proportions, and coat color.

addition, for obvious reasons, they are not good dogs to use for breeding prospective champions.

Some of the characteristics of the ideal Boxer, according to the breed standard, are as follows:

SIZE: Adult male Boxers usually stand 23 to 25 inches (58.5 to 63.5 cm) tall at the withers (the shoulder blades), while females measure 21.5 to 23.5 inches (54.5 to 60 cm). Boxers that are slightly larger or smaller than the standard will not necessarily be disqualified in a competition, but proper body proportion is important.

PROPORTION: The ideal Boxer body should be a square in profile. That is, the length from the chest to the rump should be approximately the same as the length from the top of the withers to the ground. A Boxer's musculature is balanced throughout its body, and males are bigger-boned than Boxer females.

HEAD AND MUZZLE: Judges of Boxer Conformation shows consider the proportions of head and muzzle to be of the utmost importance. The Boxer's blunt muzzle should be one-third the length of the head from the tip of the nose to the back of the skull, and two-thirds the width of the skull. The head should also be considered "clean"—without wrinkles—although wrinkles on the forehead when the ears are erect are natural and acceptable. The nose should be broad and black.

BITE AND JAW STRUCTURE: The Boxer's lower jaw should protrude beyond the upper jaw and curve slightly upward. The incisors of the lower jaw should be in a straight line, with the canine teeth in front, usually in the same line, to give the jaw an appearance of maximum width. The teeth and tongue should not show when the Boxer's mouth is shut. Generally speaking, the Boxer's face should be thick, broad, and squarish.

EYES: A Boxer's eyes are dark brown and situated at the front of the skull. They should be fairly large, but not protruding or too deeply set. The Boxer's expressive eyes, along with its wrinkled forehead when the dog is interested in something, give the breed a soulful, intelligent look.

Purebred Boxers have thick heads and powerful jaws. These characteristics came from ancestors of the Boxer breed, which were originally bred for hunting and war.

COAT OF MANY COLORS

Although usually fawn or brindle in color, Boxers often have a white underbelly and white on all four paws or just the front paws. These white parts are known as *flash*, and Boxers with them are called *flashy*.

In assessing Boxer coat colors, remember that fawn actually includes a variety of colors. A fawn Boxer can be light tan, yellow, honey-blond, mahogany, or reddish-brown. Some brindle Boxers can be so dark that they look almost black, but totally black Boxers don't exist.

Between 20 and 25 percent of purebred Boxers have white markings that cover more than one-third of their bodies. These dogs are known as white Boxers. Although white Boxers would be disqualified from Conformation shows, they still make excellent pets.

EARS: The ears perch on the highest points on the sides of the Boxer's skull. If the ears have been cropped—an operation in which parts of the ears are trimmed away, traditionally done when a Boxer is very young—they are long and tapered, and raised when the dog is alert. If the ears are left uncropped, they are medium-sized and thin, lying flat against the cheeks in repose. When a Boxer is alert, her uncropped ears will drop forward with a definite crease.

COAT: The Boxer's coat is considered by many to be one of this dog's most beautiful characteristics. It is short, shiny, smooth, and tight, revealing the breed's well-developed muscles.

COLOR: Boxers should be either fawn or brindle, but there can be considerable variation within those two colors (see "Coat of Many Colors, above). Brindle refers to anything from a light fawn color with a few black spots or stripes to such heavy black striping that the background color barely shows through. Many Boxers also have some white markings on the chest, neck, and face. However, for show purposes the color white should not exceed more than one-third of the entire coat.

TAIL: Traditionally, Boxer owners have docked, or shortened, their dog's tails. This requires a surgical operation in which most of the tail is cut off when the Boxer is still a puppy. The Boxer breed standard adopted by the AKC says that Boxers with undocked tails "should be severely penalized" in Conformation competitions. However, in recent years some Boxer owners have opted not to dock their dogs' tails.

CHARACTER AND TEMPERAMENT: The Boxer's dignified bearing is one of this dog's hallmarks. In a show ring, the dog should show restrained enthusiasm. By nature alert and self-confident, a Boxer will be playful with all family members and patient with children. This breed is wary of strangers, although Boxers typically are not aggressive without cause. If threatened, however, a Boxer will show dauntless courage and will fight to the death to protect her family.

WHAT ROLE WILL YOUR BOXER PLAY?

A Boxer can play a variety of roles, depending on her owner's preference. Boxers are superb guard dogs because of their excellent hearing. If a suspicious noise catches their sharp ears, they will bark like crazy, alerting their owners to a possible intruder. Boxers generally are not attack dogs, however. They are unlikely to maul the new mailman or jump your pastor if he stops by for a

THE NATURAL LOOK

Fewer Boxer owners are cropping their dogs' ears or docking their tails nowadays. Traditionally, a Boxer's ears were cropped, giving a classic pointy-eared look, because long floppy ears could easily be grabbed and damaged by other animals when Boxers were used for hunting and herding. Boxer tails were traditionally shortened, or docked, for similar reasons, as damage to the tail does not heal easily and can eventually affect the dog's overall health. However, these changes are expensive for owners, painful for the dogs, and can lead to infections, so growing numbers of people feel that they are unnecessary. Today fewer Boxer owners, even those who show their dogs, are having these procedures done.

Judges of Conformation events have accepted this trend. While it would have been unthinkable a decade ago to show a Boxer without cropped ears and a docked tail, today an "all-natural" Boxer is just as likely as any other to win a Best of Breed competition.

Traditionally, a Boxer's ears are cropped when she is just a few weeks old, creating the distinctive pointed look called for in the Boxer breed standard. Ear crops come in different sizes and shapes, depending on whether you plan to show your Boxer.

chat. A Boxer will look to her master to determine whom to let in the house and whom to keep out. But if a Boxer or her family is confronted or threatened, she'll put up a fierce fight, often clamping an adversary in her jaws and pulling him to the ground.

Boxers are also loyal family pets. They live to please their masters and are even-tempered and eager to learn. They take to obedience training like champs because of their keen intelligence. Boxers also get along well with children, but as with any dogs, they should be supervised when playing with toddlers (for the dog's well-being as well as the child's). Boxers are highly active, and are always up for a long walk, a run on the beach, or a game of catch with a tennis ball or a Frisbee.

FAST FACT

Boxers are—can we say this delicately?—major wind-breakers. They are gassier than many other breeds. They can't help it. If your Boxer's gassiness becomes a major problem, switching to a different brand of food may help.

Therefore, a solitary life in a small apartment is not the ideal environment for this energetic canine, and will make for a dispirited Boxer.

A Boxer will usually enjoy the company of other dogs, particularly other Boxers. What's more, having two Boxers in the home as playmates will take some of the burden off you to keep your lively canine occupied and exercised. Remember, a bored, couch-potato Boxer can become a major mischief-maker. As for cats, well, that's a bit trickier. If a Boxer puppy is brought into a home with an adult cat, the cat will usually teach the dog from the start who's the boss. However, a kitten brought into a home with a Boxer puppy or adult could be in for some rough-housing that might inadvertently harm the kitten.

All things considered, a Boxer makes an ideal family pet—smart, playful, loyal, and loving.

CHAPTER TWO

History of the Boxer Breed

The Boxer breed can be traced back to a sturdy, fearless mastiff known as the Bullenbeiser, or bull baiter. More than 4,000 years ago, ancient Assyrian warriors were known to charge onto battlefields accompanied by their Bullenbeisers; these massive-headed, powerful dogs could flatten an enemy soldier and pin him to the ground until the dog's master could move in for the kill. The Assyrians also hunted with their Bullenbeisers, as the dogs could catch and hold bears, boars, and other prey. And like today's Boxer, the Bullenbeiser could also herd cattle and guard his master's home.

The Bullenbeiser is now extinct, but his distant relatives live on as the Boxers you see competing on

The modern Boxer breed was developed in Germany during the 19th century.

televised dog shows or as the Boxer companions lying at their masters' feet. In the modern Boxer's agility, strength, courage, and intelligence, you can still see traces of the mighty Bullenbeiser.

THE MODERN BOXER

The first modern Boxer was born in Germany in the 1830s, the offspring of a Brabanter Bullenbeiser (a smaller version of the German Bullenbeiser) and an English Bulldog. German breeders and owners of Bullenbeisers imported a bulldog named Tom from England. Tom was mostly white, but the Bullenbeiser he was mated with was brindle-colored. Their offspring had the distinctive look of the modern Boxer—a dark coat with a white underbelly. The first Boxer recorded in the German studbook (and, for all intents and purposes, the official first Boxer) was named Flocki, son of Tom. A new breed had arrived, and soon it would spread throughout the world.

The first Boxer club was organized in Germany in 1896, and in that

ORIGIN OF THE BREED'S NAME

There are several theories about how the Boxer breed came by its name. Unfortunately, the most interesting of these theories is the least likely to be true. That one holds that the Boxer is so named because of these dogs' tendency to stand on their back legs and "throw punches" when they get in a fight. However, Boxer historians doubt that Germans would have chosen an English word to name their favorite dog.

A more likely theory is that the name comes from the word *boxl*, which in the Bavarian dialect of the German language means "short leather pants or underwear" and could describe the Boxer's color pattern. *Boxl* was also a term used to

When playing or fighting, Boxers sometimes throw up their front paws as though they were punching an opponent.

describe the Bullenbeiser, and the word could have been twisted to become Boxer.

same year the first Boxers were registered and the first Boxer show held. For the next 50 years, Germans would lead the way in Boxer breeding and development, establishing a breed standard in 1902. From 1902 to 1911, the breed soared in popularity. German breeders worked to refine the Boxer, weeding out undesirable physical and behavioral traits.

FRAU STOCKMANN, GODMOTHER OF THE MODERN BOXER

One woman had an enormous influence on the development of the Boxer breed. Frau Friederun Stockmann was an artist and sculptor who also was crazy about Boxers. In fact, Frau Stockmann was so nuts about the breed that her autobiography was titled *My Life with Boxers*. She bred and showed her champion Boxers through two world wars and even trained the dogs to help in the war effort. There was no one more familiar with the Boxer's abilities—its agility, stamina, intelligence, and courage.

Frau Stockmann's husband, Phillip, was also an artist and Boxer lover. When he was drafted to serve in World War I, he took most of his Boxers to the Western Front with him. Boxers worked alongside their soldier handlers performing a variety of tasks: tracking the enemy, rooting out and attacking snipers, carrying messages across enemy lines, and often even charging into battle with the German army.

One Boxer in particular, named CH Roll von Vogelsberg, received special commendations for his bravery under fire. Working with a German patrol unit, he would surprise and round up groups of enemy soldiers, all by himself, then hold them until reinforcements arrived. Miraculously, this fearless Boxer survived the First World War and lived out his remaining days in comfort, receiving letters of praise from across the globe.

Ironically, considering her effort for the German war machine in World War I, Frau Stockmann also exerted a great influence on the Boxer breed in the United States. Although she was able to keep her Von Dom ("Of the Cathedral") Kennels from being destroyed through two devastating wars, Frau Stockmann had to make sacrifices to do this. Strapped for money, her nation and its economy in tatters, she had to sell some of her best Boxers to breeders in the United States and Canada to support the other dogs in her kennel. Although this was a heartbreaking loss to Frau Stockmann, it was a great boon to the Boxer breed in North America. Frau Stockmann's Boxers and their descendants helped bring the breed to prominence in the United States, and Boxers have grown more and more popular each year.

COMING TO NORTH AMERICA

There was a buzz in the audience at the Westminster Kennel Club Show of 1898. It was the first time many of the dog-savvy people in attendance had seen this new German breed called the Boxer. That year two Boxers trotted into an American dog show ring for the first time. Boxers appeared again at a show in Chicago in 1902. But it wasn't until 1915 that the United States had its first Boxer champion. Dampf von Dom (yes, of Frau Stockmann's Von Dom Kennels), a German import who had won many prizes in Europe, took his first American title under the proud gaze of owner Herbert H. Lehman, the future governor of New York.

By the 1930s, the dog world in the United States was changing, with dog shows becoming more professional and breed standards more formalized. In 1936, obedience regulations were adopted, and professional handlers were required to be licensed. The American Kennel Club

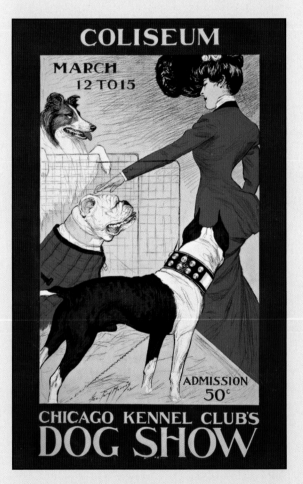

A Boxer is one of the three dogs being admired by a well-dressed woman in this promotional poster for a Chicago dog show. The poster dates from 1902, soon after the breed was introduced in America, indicating the high level of interest in Boxers.

had been stung by the fact that most of the winning dogs in American shows were from Europe, so the club offered money to American breeders to produce championship stock. So breeders set to work with renewed enthusiasm, and that included Boxer breeders. In 1935 the American Boxer Club was formed, signaling that Boxers had finally established their bona fides on this side of the Atlantic.

After World War II, Americans and Canadians, flush with victory and having time and money to spare, turned much of their attention to their dogs and to the tasks of breeding and showing their favorites. By 1946 the Boxer had become the fifth most popular dog breed in the United States. For three straight years, American-bred Boxers won Best in Show at the Westminster Kennel Club show in New York, boosting the breed's popularity even more.

In 1949, the first superstar of North American Boxers was born—Bang Away of Sirrah Crest. Ten years earlier, Dr. R. C. Harris and his wife, Phoebe, had started Sirrah ("Harris" spelled backwards) Crest Kennels in California, unaware that they would eventually breed the winningest Boxer ever. Even as a puppy, Bang Away was pronounced

great by none other than Frau Stockmann herself, who was visiting the United States at the time. Through the 1950s Bang Away became so popular that his face graced the covers of national magazines, and when he traveled to shows by air, he often rode in the cockpit with the pilots. Many breeders believe that Bang Away was directly responsible for the lean, long-muzzled look still popular in North American and British Boxers.

Today the Boxer is sixth on the list of favorite dogs in the United States and eighth on the list of Canada's favorite canines, proving that North America's love affair with the Boxer is holding fast.

In the United Kingdom, as in North America, the Boxer's popularity soared after the Second World War. Many British soldiers had seen German Boxers performing admirably in police and military work

FAST FACT

The long "show" crop of a Boxer's ears, still seen in American Conformation, is now banned in England and Germany. The trend in the United States is also slowly moving away from cropping ears and docking tails.

Purebred German Boxers, like the one shown above, are larger and exhibit slightly different physical characteristics than their American and British cousins.

during the war, and the Brits brought their admiration home, where it quickly spread. Allon Dawson, who founded the Northern Boxer Club near Leeds, was one of the first breeders dedicated to producing British Boxers. Like his North American counterparts, Dawson founded his kennel with dogs from the bloodline of Frau Stockmann's Boxers.

Allon Dawson was also one of the first officers of the British Boxer Club and played a role in developing the British breed standard. Dawson would have liked the breed standard to reflect his preference in Boxer physiques, however. Dawson was a big fan of the stout, Bulldog-like German Boxer, but after much debate, British Boxer clubs eventually adopted a breed standard very similar to the standards in the United States and Canada—that is, the lean, sleek, and longer-muzzled Boxer.

Interestingly, while Boxer breed standards are now comparable in the United States, the United Kingdom,

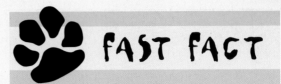

FAST FACT

More than 35,000 Boxers are registered in the United States every year.

and Canada, the Boxer in Germany remains a breed apart. In Germany the breed standard is still heavily influenced by the Boxer's continuing role as a working dog, mainly in police and military operations, as well as in search and rescue. Therefore, German Boxers are bigger-boned and more heavily muscled than their British and North American cousins. They also have broader heads, shorter muzzles, and a more powerful bite. However, the North American and British breed standards are considered the more popular standards internationally, perhaps because they are more aesthetically pleasing, and North America is now generally regarded as the center of the Boxer-breeding universe.

CHAPTER THREE

Being a Responsible Pet Owner

When you decided to bring a dog into your life, you made a solemn promise to care for your canine friend. As a dog owner you're expected to provide healthy, nourishing food at proper intervals; fresh drinking water regularly; comfortable, safe surroundings; proper health care; and a reasonable amount of exercise and fun. In return, your dog will defend you with her life.

But dog owners have a responsibility to their communities, too. For example, as a dog owner, you're obligated to keep your dog from becoming a nuisance by barking incessantly. You are also obligated to make sure your dog never harms any

Your Boxer should always wear an identification tag that includes your phone number.

person or another animal. No biting is allowed, except under exceptional circumstances, and you must always keep her rabies vaccines and other shots up-to-date. You're obligated to see that your dog is either fenced in or leashed so she doesn't decide to bury her chew toy in the neighbor's vegetable garden. You're also required to clean up after your dog if she makes a mess in public places or on anyone else's property.

IDENTIFICATION

Another of your obligations to both dog and community is to make sure your Boxer is properly identified so that she may be returned to you, should she ever get lost. The easiest way to do this, of course, is with a tag attached to her collar that carries her name and your phone number. Be sure to include the area code, because dogs can travel very far indeed when they're lost and confused.

Tags can be lost or deliberately removed, however, so more permanent means of identification have been developed as well. It's a good idea to identify your boxer in more than one way. Two common forms of dog ID are permanent tattoos and microchips.

TATTOOS: Recently, more and more dog owners have been tattooing their

FAST FACT

Dog identification tags can quickly become tarnished or worn and illegible. Check them every month or two to make sure they can still be read.

dogs. The tattoo consists of a number imprinted on the inside of the dog's thigh, and that number goes into a national tattoo registry. This has proven quite effective in returning lost dogs to their owners. The procedure is not painful, and the dog can be conscious through the whole process. If you tattoo your Boxer as a puppy, however, the tattooed number may become illegible as she grows. Keep an eye on her tattoo if you're relying on that as her backup ID, and make sure you can read it whenever you check for it.

MICROCHIPS: Also gaining in popularity is the practice of microchipping a dog to aid in identification. In this procedure your vet, usually in one of your initial visits with your new dog, will ask if you'd like your dog chipped for a small additional fee, usually $25 to $50. If you agree to this, the vet will quickly insert a small microchip about the size of a grain of rice

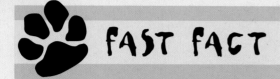

under the dog's skin between her shoulder blades. The dog feels a brief pinch and then she's good to go. If she's ever lost, she can be checked with a special scanner (available at most vets' offices and shelters) and instantly identified.

Microchip identification has become very popular, but it's not without drawbacks. For example, only vets and shelters have scanners, so a person who finds your lost Boxer without her tag may not know to check for a chip. Also, in some dogs, the chips can shift from their original location between the shoulder blades to some other part of the body where the scanner can't read them. Finally, one recent study seems to indicate that dogs implanted with microchips may be more prone to developing tumors in the implant area.

LICENSING

Many states and municipalities require that all dogs be licensed. This is meant to protect citizens from irresponsible pet owners and vicious or stray dogs. To get a license, a dog owner just needs to fill out an application, provide proof that the dog has been vaccinated against rabies, and pay a small fee. Sometimes, the fee is reduced or waived for dogs that have been spayed or neutered. To find out about your own area's requirements, call your city or county clerk's office or your state's department of agriculture. Your vet should be thoroughly familiar with local requirements as well.

SPAYING OR NEUTERING YOUR DOG

One trip to your nearest animal shelter will convince you of the need to spay or neuter domestic animals. But even if you think you might want to breed your Boxer eventually, it's important to weigh the pros and cons to determine whether it's better to spay or neuter your Boxer or to keep the dog intact.

Truthfully, there are very few good reasons not to spay or neuter your dog. If you intend to enter your Boxer in Conformation events, you really don't have the option. The purpose of these shows is to evaluate breeding stock, so dogs that participate must be intact. If you have a show-quality Boxer and you would

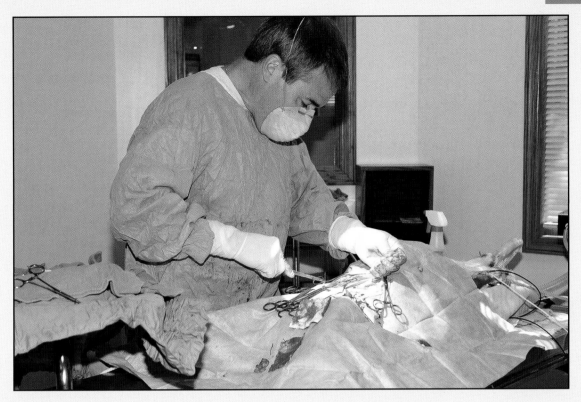

For most people, spaying or neutering their dog is the right thing to do.

like to continue her champion bloodline, then it's certainly your right to breed your dog.

However, keeping your Boxer intact will make living with him or her much more difficult. For example, an intact male, from the age of six months on, will sense any female dog in heat, anywhere in your neighborhood. And he'll do whatever it takes to reach her. This means he'll bolt when you open the front door, climb the highest fence you can build, and dig a tunnel to get out of any backyard. If a female in heat walks past your house, your male Boxer will anxiously hurl himself against the front window.

On the other hand, neutering a male Boxer provides a number of benefits. It will make him less aggressive, as well as less likely to exhibit undesirable sexually driven behaviors, such as marking territory with urine or roaming in search of a female. It will also reduce or eliminate his risk of contracting some diseases, including testicular cancer and prostate cancer. The neutering procedure is relatively simple, and, contrary to a common myth, it will not change your Boxer's personality.

A Boxer that gets loose is a danger to others and to herself, so your backyard must have a high and sturdy fence. Alternately, electric fences are usually effective at keeping your Boxer close to home; however, they may not be deterrent enough to prevent an intact male from chasing a female in heat.

An unspayed female Boxer will be a magnet for every intact male in her vicinity. She runs the risk of being impregnated just by going into her own backyard. Also, intact females often have a messy, bloody discharge approximately twice a year during their heat cycles.

Spaying your female Boxer will eliminate her risk of developing ovarian or uterine cancer, and will greatly reduce her risk of mammary tumors. It will eliminate her messy heat cycles, and will also alleviate the mood swings that intact females typically experience.

Dogs can be spayed or neutered at six months of age or even younger. Check with your vet to see at what age he would recommend the procedure. While spaying is a more complicated operation than neutering, every vet in the country performs both so often that the procedures are routine. The bottom line is that, in most cases, a spayed or neutered

Boxer is a happier Boxer. You'll be a happier owner, too.

PET INSURANCE

With so many humans uninsured in the United States, it seems a luxury to even think about pet insurance, but let's just look at this option. Is it a good investment?

Veterinary science has made great advances in pet care over the past decade. Procedures once available only to humans are now being performed on dogs. For example, bone-marrow transplants are now being done to extend the lives of canines with certain cancers. As you might imagine, these procedures do not come cheap. Pet insurance can sometimes help defray the costs.

However (and this is a big however), many of the most serious dog illnesses occur when the dog is older. Typically, pet insurance companies will not cover older dogs, even if they covered the same dog when she was young. Also, with pet insurance, as with human insurance, there are deductibles, exclusions, and caps on payments. For example, several prominent pet insurance companies will not cover treatments for hip dysplasia in breeds that are prone to that disease.

Plus, like veterinary care, pet insurance has a hefty price tag. Typically it can run from $2,000 to $5,000 over the life of your dog. You can pay a lot of vet bills out-of-pocket for that kind of money. Still, if you're the type of pet owner who will do almost anything to give your beloved dog a little more time, pet insurance might be a good idea. Other dog owners might feel that quality of life is more important than quantity and opt not to perform desperate, heroic, and expensive procedures.

The good news is that responsible pet owners can forestall many serious illnesses by making sure their dogs get timely, preventive health care throughout their lives. They can also keep their pets safe by always using a leash when they're outside of a fenced area.

LEGAL ISSUES

The laws regarding dog ownership are simple: you cannot allow your

Your local municipality's animal control office may have a Web site that lists the ordinances and legal requirements related to dog ownership.

dog to become a nuisance or a threat to people or other animals. If you do, you can be held legally accountable. The nuisance category can include a dog that roams the neighborhood, overturning garbage cans, digging holes in others' yards, or attacking other pets. You may also get a visit from the police if your dog barks incessantly, especially at night. In many communities, you can be fined for not picking up after your dog when she eliminates in public.

If your dog becomes a threat to others, then you may face serious legal problems. The law takes dog bites seriously. If your dog attacks and seriously injures someone, you'll probably be facing a hefty fine and might even go to prison. At the very

least, your Boxer could be branded a "vicious dog" and put down by the authorities. You could also be sued by the victim and would likely have your homeowner's insurance canceled.

Since potential dog bites are by far the most serious legal issue a dog owner can face, it pays to review the things you can do to lessen the chances that your dog will ever bite:

- Make sure your dog gets lots of exercise. An exhausted dog is a happy dog, and a happy dog doesn't bite.

- Don't leave kids alone with your dog.

- Neuter your male dog. He'll be less aggressive.

- Enroll your dog in obedience classes and complete them.

- If you see a neighbor or someone else teasing your dog, put a stop to it immediately.

CANINE GOOD CITIZEN

Responsible pet ownership is so important that both the American

NO BITING!

Following are some tips that will help prevent your Boxer from biting a person or another dog:

- train and socialize her
- never let your Boxer off her leash unless in a designated off-leash area
- watch your Boxer carefully, especially when she is around children
- if a stranger approaches while you and your pet are walking, move out of his way, especially if your dog starts to get her hackles up
- post warning signs on your property to keep strangers from approaching your Boxer

Kennel Club and the Kennel Club of the United Kingdom have created programs to promote responsible dog ownership for all dog owners, not just the owners of purebreds. The AKC's Canine Good Citizen Test was developed in 1989 to encourage dog owners to teach their pets proper behavior. The Kennel Club of the United Kingdom implemented a similar test, called the Good Citizen Dog Scheme, in 1992.

FAST FACT

Never chain your dog in the yard. This only increases frustration and anger, making her more likely to bite.

The purpose of the Canine Good Citizen program is to recognize dogs with great manners. Today, it's the basis for many other AKC-sponsored activities, including Agility and Obedience competitions, and most therapy organizations require dogs to pass the CGC test. There are other advantages to Canine Good Citizen certification as well. CGC dogs may be allowed in certain business establishments, such as hotels, that otherwise prohibit dogs.

The Canine Good Citizen Test is a non-competitive, pass-or-fail test that consists of 10 elements, as follows:

ACCEPTING A FRIENDLY STRANGER: Your Boxer must remain well behaved, showing no fear, shyness, or guarding, when a stranger approaches and shakes your hand. Sitting politely for petting: While sitting beside you, your Boxer must be willing to accept being petted and touched by a stranger.

APPEARANCE AND GROOMING: Your Boxer must allow a stranger to brush her, pick up each foot for examination, and check inside her ears. She cannot show any signs of aggression or shyness during this process.

WALK ON A LOOSE LEASH: Your dog must walk beside you on a loose leash while making turns and stops.

WALK THROUGH A CROWD: Your Boxer must remain calm while walking through a crowd of people. She's allowed to show interest in the people, but she cannot jump, pull, or act fearful.

SIT AND DOWN ON COMMAND; STAY IN PLACE: Your dog must sit

Only well-trained Boxers can earn the AKC's Canine Good Citizen certification.

and lie down when you give her the commands to do so. You're allowed to give your Boxer the command more than once and use more than one word—a phrase is acceptable. She must then remain in the sit or down position while you walk 20 feet (6 m) away and then back to your dog.

COME WHEN CALLED: With your dog in a stay, or with the evaluator distracting your dog by petting her, walk 10 feet (3 m) away from your Boxer, then call her to come. She must come to you.

REACTION TO ANOTHER DOG: You and your dog will walk up to another person and his dog. You'll stop, shake hands, and have a brief conversation. During this interaction, your Boxer should show no more than a passing interest in the other dog. You and your dog then walk away. Neither dog can show shyness or aggression.

REACTION TO DISTRACTION: During simulated everyday situations, your Boxer must remain calm. She can show a natural curiosity and be a little startled, but she cannot show aggression, panic, or fear.

SUPERVISED SEPARATION: Your Boxer proves that she can be well behaved when left alone for three minutes with another person.

Training and testing for the AKC's Canine Good Citizen Test are offered at many dog-training facilities. The American Kennel Club's Web site, www.akc.org, provides a list of registered evaluators.

❧❧❧

When you welcome a dog into your life, you also assume the very important job of socializing that dog and making sure she's a good pet, a good neighbor, and a good canine citizen. You'll be held responsible if she goes astray. However, because of the Boxer's willingness to please her master, your job of making her an enjoyable animal to have around should be relatively easy—if you start early and take the task of training her (and yourself) seriously.

chapter four

The Best Start for You and Your Dog

If you've read this far, you have probably already decided to add a Boxer to your family. Next, it's time to decide what type of Boxer is right for you. This is not as simple as it sounds. For example, you'll have a far different Boxer experience if you get a bouncing male puppy from a breeder than if you adopt a mature female Boxer from a shelter. Neither one is inherently better than the other, but one will

Before you bring a Boxer into your home, your entire family must get involved in preparing the living area and establishing rules that the newcomer will be expected to follow.

undoubtedly be a better fit for you and your family.

MALE OR FEMALE?

Few things are purely black and white (not even the brindle Boxer!), so the sex-related differences you're about to read here are general tendencies based on the experience of many dog owners. Any particular male or female dog may deviate from the norm, of course.

People who have owned both male and female Boxers say that, as a rule, female Boxers are more stubborn and willful. If they set their minds to something, they're not easily dissuaded. Also, according to some Boxer owners, females don't easily forgive or forget a slight or indignity they imagine they have suffered. They may later exact revenge by hiding their owner's shoe, for example (hey, Boxers are smart).

Male Boxers, on the other hand, usually defer to their masters in everything, often following their owners from room to room, even if it's just a short trip to the kitchen to get a drink of water. A male Boxer may be more likely to curl at your feet while you read a book and

Boxers can make great pets whether they are female (left) or male.

probably won't hide your loafers even after you've disciplined him.

However, before you start thinking that male Boxers have it all over females, take note: the male Boxer is big and strong and full of energy. Do you have the strength to walk and train him? If not, you might be better off with the smaller, slightly more docile female. Also, like any male dog, a male Boxer will seek to mark his territory by lifting his leg and urinating on it. And even though you pay the mortgage, your house (and your furniture) are his territory.

The female, though, has problems of her own. Starting when she's about a year old, she'll have twice-yearly heat cycles, which last about three weeks each. During these times she'll leak a messy discharge and must be allowed outside only under careful supervision to prevent an unwanted pregnancy. Pet supply stores sell diaperlike wraps a female can wear during her cycle to minimize staining around the house.

Both of these sex-related problems can be curtailed or eliminated by spaying or neutering your pet. In fact, unless you're a professional breeder, there's no reason not to spay or neuter your Boxer. Shelters throughout the world are full of "accidental" puppies.

PUPPY OR MATURE DOG?

Almost everyone loves puppies. With their big eyes and big heads, their little bitty bodies and doofy antics and sloppy kisses, they are ready-made Disney characters. And therein lies the trap. Puppies are indeed adorable, and their antics can keep their owners entertained for hours each day. But, according to the American Boxer Rescue Association, thousands of these once-cute little buggers end up in shelters and at Boxer rescue locations every year. Why? Because they were bought on impulse or purchased by someone who did not give careful thought to how much work a puppy could be. Bringing a puppy into your home will require a significant change in your lifestyle.

You and your household may already be puppy-ready, but it's still appropriate to remind you of what might be in store. First of all, puppies need to be trained, and while Boxers are one of the most easily trained

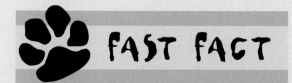

FAST FACT

One of the most playful and jovial breeds, Boxers usually act like puppies for most of their lives.

breeds, some dogs take to training better than others. Training requires a daily commitment of your time and effort until your puppy understands the basic commands: "come," "sit," "down," and "stay." If you want to spice up the routine a bit, you can also add "shake," "roll over," or whatever else you can think up to keep you and your pup amused. But teaching just the basics can take weeks or months of daily practice.

Training is absolutely necessary, though. An untrained dog is pain to live with or even to encounter in passing.

Then there's the issue of house-training. One thing you can definitely count on: your puppy will have accidents in the house. If you have expensive Oriental rugs, you'll need to roll them up for a few months. You'll also need to buy cleaning supplies and a mop.

Puppies are playful, and because Boxer puppies belong to a high-energy breed, they're more playful than most. They will leap off furniture, knock over lamps, and

crash into walls. At times you may feel as if you spend your whole day trying to keep your romping puppy from hurting herself. This activity is perfectly natural, however; you just have to ride it out while keeping puppy and household in one piece.

Just like human babies, puppies will go through a teething stage. For

A spindly legged Boxer puppy is extremely cute, but he'll require careful supervision and training to keep him out of trouble.

this time you want to make sure you have plenty of sturdy dog chew toys around and that your puppy knows that they are hers. Likewise, let her know that your furniture is *not* hers to chew. She must also learn not to chew on fingers.

Finally, with a puppy in the house (or a dog of any age, for that matter), you'll have to adjust your lifestyle. You can no longer just jet off to the Bahamas for a weekend without arranging care for your dog. She'll also need to be walked at least two or three times a day (more for puppies), so if you work outside the house, you'll need to make arrangements for that as well.

Have you been talked out of a puppy yet? Let's hope not, because puppies can be great dynamos of joy, too. There are many benefits to getting a puppy. First, your puppy is, figuratively, a lump of clay for you to mold. In many ways, your dog's adult personality will depend on you. Like a child, your puppy will learn from you how to work, how to relax, and how to love. With help and kindness from everyone in the family, you can turn your rowdy pup into a wonderful family pet you'll enjoy for years to come. She'll become as much a part of your home as any family member.

You can also help ensure your puppy's future health by being careful about her nutrition and exercise, and being sure she's properly immunized at the appropriate ages.

Finally, the intangibles. A puppy will light up her new home with her boundless enthusiasm and zest for life. She may even add years to her master's life by insisting that he

DETERMINING YOUR PUPPY'S APTITUDE

The potential for a puppy to fill any specific role has been turned into something of a science. Jack and Wendy Volhard, well-respected dog trainers and authors, have devised the Puppy Aptitude Test to make it easier to evaluate puppies. The test, in its entirety, can be viewed on their Web site, www.volhard.com. Psychologist and canine intelligence expert Stanley Coren developed both a Canine IQ Test and an Obedience Personality Test, which are outlined in his book *The Intelligence of Dogs*. If you have specific goals for your Boxer puppy, consider evaluating him using one or more of these methods.

accompany her on long brisk walks around the neighborhood.

On the other hand, adopting an adult Boxer might be best for you. While it's true that you'll miss the goofy antics and bubbly inquisitiveness of the puppy, you'll also be able to skip housetraining, mess-cleaning, and furniture-replacing (few puppies will actually eat the whole dining table). With an adult dog, you've got a ready-made companion, often one that is so grateful to have a home that she'll do anything to please you. Adopting a mature dog might be best for people who work days and for older people who don't necessarily want to try to keep up with a puppy. Most adult Boxers will already be at least partially trained.

To find an adult Boxer, check your local shelter, or look in the phone book or online to find the nearest Boxer rescue organization. Boxer rescue groups note that thousands of Boxers are given up each year, some because their masters have moved or passed on, and others because their owners didn't want a dog as much as they thought. Regardless, don't assume that a Boxer left at a shelter has some sort of personality disorder. Often it's the ex-owner who had the problem. To be sure if a mature dog is right for you, ask if you can take one home

for a night or two to see how the two of you get along. Most shelters have areas where the dogs can run and play. Go outside with your prospective canine pal and have some fun. You may fall in love on the spot.

Another advantage of adopting an adult dog is that her personality, temperament, and abilities will be fully developed. So if you're looking to show your Boxer or compete in sports like Agility or Flyball, you won't have to guess whether a particular Boxer has the right stuff: you can see for yourself.

FINDING A RESPONSIBLE BREEDER

If you've decided to go the puppy route, how do you find a good one? There are reputable, responsible, quality breeders who produce excellent dogs, but there are also many backyard breeders who are just in the business to make a few bucks.

A quality Boxer breeder will breed puppies that adhere closely to the Standard of Perfection. Dogs from a quality breeder will often be of show caliber because their parents or grandparents were show dogs. A reputable breeder will breed only Boxers with desirable characteristics of temperament, namely, obedience, kindness, and curiosity.

Likewise, dogs that aren't 100 percent healthy will not be bred.

Specifically, a Boxer pup's parents should be free from hip dysplasia (ask to see the certification number from the Orthopedic Foundation for Animals or PennHIP) and Boxer cardiomyopathy. A good breeder's dogs should also be certified as having no visual abnormalities by the Canine Eye Registration Foundation (CERF). In addition, purebred puppies should be registered with the American Kennel Club or other appropriate organization, depending on the country where the owner lives.

Besides giving you some confidence that your new Boxer is healthy, a quality breeder will also give you a written guarantee of the pup's health. If your puppy develops a serious health problem once you get her home, the breeder will take the dog back and either give you a new puppy or refund your money. This guarantee, from a good breeder, should apply regardless of the dog's age.

FAST FACT

If you adopt a Boxer from a Boxer rescue organization, make sure to send the rescue group a picture of your dog in her new home. Most shelters and rescue facilities keep scrapbooks of their success stories.

As a prospective Boxer owner, you shouldn't think this interview process is a one-way street, however. A serious breeder will also want to know that his quality puppies will be going to quality homes. He may ask you about other family members, their ages, and whether they love dogs. He will ask if you have a fenced-in backyard or someplace else nearby where your Boxer can get the exercise she needs. He may also insist that you give your puppy proper nutrition and health care. As you can see, there are many reasons to choose a top-notch breeder.

Okay, so what if you're just looking for a companion dog and aren't interested in ever showing your Boxer? Can you get a good dog for less money from a backyard breeder? Sure, it happens all the time. You'll be assuming more risks than you might want to assume, though. Vet bills are expensive, and if your little pup isn't healthy, or if she has temperament problems and turns into a biter, you'll be paying a lot more later for not being cautious at the start.

HOW TO FIND THE EXCEPTIONAL BREEDER

Imagine that you're lost in a strange city without a map. You know your destination, but you don't know how to get there. What do you do? Of course, you ask someone who lives there and knows the area. It's the same with finding a good breeder. Grab the phone book and look up a nearby veterinarian whom you might end up using once you get your pet. If the vet doesn't know of any local Boxer breeders, he'll be able to point you to others who do know. Also, the United States Boxer Association (USBA) is a repository of breed information. When you contact representatives of the USBA (addresses, phone numbers, and Web sites of many useful organizations appear under Organizations to Contact in the back of this book), tell them

what you're looking for in your Boxer—a show dog, a companion, or a working dog. They will be able to recommend breeders who specialize.

You can also attend dog shows and approach the owners or handlers of Boxers before or after the show to ask about good breeders. (A note of caution: It's best not to approach an owner or handler during the show. A lot of dog people get pretty uptight during competitions, and their reactions might not be positive.)

As a prospective dog owner, it's not generally advisable to peruse the classifieds of the local paper in search of a Boxer breeder, but you can certainly check the ads in the

PAPERS YOUR BREEDER SHOULD SUPPLY

American Kennel Club registration papers—These are necessary to register the dog or puppy in your name.

Puppy sale contract—Reputable breeders issue puppy sale contracts to help ensure the welfare of the puppies they sell. The advantages for puppy buyers is that these contracts help avoid misunderstandings by outlining the responsibilities of both the breeder and the buyer, and they note, in writing, any health guarantees.

Pedigree—This is a chart of the dog's or puppy's family tree. The availability of this information shows that the breeder is serious about keeping meticulous records of her breeding program.

Health records—These should document any veterinary care your dog or puppy has received, including vaccinations, wormings, medications and surgeries.

breed magazine, *The Boxer Review*. While not every breeder listed there is a quality breeder, you can visit the Web sites of the ones that seem to fit the bill and work from there.

When you find your Boxer breeder, and you've checked out his facility and are satisfied that it's clean and that his dogs seem happy, active, and well treated, tell him exactly what you're looking for in a Boxer. He knows his dogs, their strengths and weaknesses, and he'll want to match up the right dog with the right owner. Don't be disappointed if you have to wait a while for a puppy. Many breeders breed only at certain times of the year, so you might have to put a deposit down on a dog that isn't even born yet. This should not be discouraging. On the contrary, it's a good indication that you've found a very good breeder.

If this seems like a lot of work, it is. Keep in mind, though, that your new puppy is an investment in the future for both of you. You want to make that future as bright as it can possibly be.

MEETING YOUR PUPPY

When it's time to meet the companion who might be sharing the next ten or fifteen years of your life with you, you might feel a little nervous. This is understandable. It's almost like a first date, and you want things to go well. Like a first date, however, you don't want to be too eager. There are certain traits, apparent even in

When evaluating a litter of Boxer puppies, watch to see how they interact with each other, as well as with members of your family.

puppies, for which you'll be on the lookout and other traits you'll want to avoid.

A great way to begin is to sit down with the pups and let them come to you. Pet and play with each one, paying close attention to how they all interact with you and with each other. A good breeder will probably explain to you what he has already discerned about their personalities. You should listen to him, but the decision is still yours. Does one pup seem more drawn to you than the others? This is important. As in any relationship, you should never underestimate the power of chemistry. It may be hard to choose, so rely on your intuition. Does one dog feel more "right" to you than any of the others?

As for temperament, it's usually best to choose the middle course, especially if you're adopting your Boxer as a companion animal. The best pup is a pup that is not too shy or fearful; timidity can be hard to overcome in a dog, and sometimes leads to fear-induced biting. Nor do you want the boldest, baddest pup in the litter. You don't want to live with a bully, especially if you have other pets that must get along with the newcomer. In general, you should choose the puppy that is alert, that doesn't mind being

picked up by you, and that's eager to play with both humans and with her littermates. This pup will grow into an adult dog that's eager to please, easily trained, and pleasantly companionable.

If you plan to show or compete with your Boxer, it's a good idea to consider pups whose parents excelled in Conformation events or particular activities, such as Obedience or Agility competitions. In that case, a dog with a bit of an attitude might be your best choice.

Remember to ask to see the pup's parents' papers to make sure that they are free of the three main problems that plague Boxers (hip dysplasia, Boxer cardiomyopathy, and eye disease). You should also, of course, check out the pup himself. Part the fur on her back with your fingers to check for fleas or ticks.

FAST FACT

Find out from the breeder what kind of kibble or other food your puppy has been eating before you take him home. Abrupt changes in diet can cause diarrhea. The breeder may give you a small bag of the puppy's food, to cover you for the first night or two until you can get to a pet-supply store.

There should be none. Also, check out the coat itself. There shouldn't be any bald patches (these could indicate a number of serious skin conditions, including mange), and the fur should be smooth and sleek.

Is the puppy's skin pink and healthy looking? You shouldn't see any patches or red spots. Also, look at her ears, nose, and anus. They should be free of discharges that could indicate a sick or soon-to-be sick pup.

Likewise, check the puppy's eyes. Are they bright and clear, and do they look back at you without any wandering of one eye or the other? Is she cross-eyed?

Finally, put your puppy down and let her walk and run. Is her gait even and balanced, without any legs appearing shorter than the others? Does the pup seem gimpy?

If all these things check out, you have found yourself a canine companion! Congratulations! May you have a long and happy life together.

CHOOSING A VETERINARIAN

Even though you have done everything humanly possible to bring home a healthy puppy, you'll still need to select a vet for your dog's immunizations, regular veterinary care, and possible emergencies. If you have had another pet, you probably already have a vet you like and trust. If your new pup is your first pet, you'll have to do a little research (though not nearly as much as you did in selecting a breeder, because you can always change vets).

If the breeder from whom you purchased your pup is in your town, ask him which vet he uses. This can be very handy because the vet will know not only your new dog, but most of your dog's blood relatives, too. But if your breeder lives far away, you'll need to start from scratch. A simple and very good way to get a recommendation is to ask your dog-owning neighbors what vet they use. Generally, people choose a veterinary hospital that's fairly close to home. This makes sense for the sake of convenience, and also in case you encounter an emergency situation with your pet.

If you have chosen a new vet, call and schedule a brief interview and tour of the facilities. Make sure work areas, exam rooms, and kennels (if they're available) are clean and tidy. When you speak with the vet, ask about his qualifications. You should also find out if his clinic is a member of the American Animal Hospital Association (AAHA). The certificate of membership, as well as the doctor's veterinary degree, will probably be posted in the waiting room. These

Ideally, your veterinarian should be a member of the American Animal Hospital Association. AAHA-sanctioned doctors and their clinics are held to a high standard and can be expected to provide excellent care.

inquiries will not offend the right vet. After all, your pet is like your child—that is, she relies on you for everything—and you would certainly check out a pediatrician carefully.

PUPPY-PROOFING YOUR HOME

Before you bring your puppy home, you'll have to make your home safe for her. Look at things this way: if you can get to something easily, so can your new puppy, but she'll

employ her famous Boxer curiosity by putting it in her mouth and chomping down. If curiosity killed the cat, it can also kill your puppy unless you take proper precautions.

Puppy-proofing your home can be fun if you make it a family project. Kids, especially, will get a kick out of it. Everyone should get down on the floor on hands and knees and prowl around like a puppy. What do you see? Electrical cords. Your puppy will chew these, so hide them or make then inaccessible in some other way. The same goes for small children's toys and anything mouth-sized.

Your Boxer will likely want to check out whatever is on top of low tables and shelves, so make sure there's nothing at eye level (remember, you're on hands and knees now) that's breakable or could be swallowed. Don't tempt your new friend by leaving shoes in her path, especially of the fuzzy slipper kind. A puppy can't tell the difference

FAST FACT

Boxers are extremely clever and will often figure out how to open doors, latches, cabinets, and drawers. You can stop them by puppy-proofing your home with childproof locks.

between her fuzzy toy and a slipper that looks just like it.

Until your puppy is housebroken, it's wise to roll up expensive rugs and cover upholstery. Even more important, you'll want to lock away (in a basement, a garage, or a locked cabinet) any cleaning products, pesticides, and garden supplies. Remember, just because a product comes in a childproof container does not mean a Boxer can't get into it. Most household products are as toxic to pets as they are to people (sometimes even more so).

Medicines, too, should be kept well out of your Boxer's reach.

Finally, take out the trash or put it in a locked cabinet. Boxers have an incredible sense of smell, and the remains of last night's dinner will seem mighty appealing to a puppy, even one that's well fed. Chicken bones, bottle caps, and paper or plastic bags can get lodged in a puppy's throat and kill her in moments.

Ultimately, though, almost all the difficulties you'll encounter bringing your new puppy home can be eliminated by confining her to one safe room, at least for the first few weeks.

Most dog bites occur in the home, and children are often the ones who are bitten. Make sure your new puppy or adult Boxer is always supervised around children.

SUPPLIES YOU'LL NEED

You have probably already discovered that owning a dog can be an expensive proposition, but supplies are one thing on which you can save a little money. If you had another dog before, one that was approximately the same size, there's nothing wrong with recycling bowls, crates, leashes, or even toys. You're not forgetting your previous dog or besmirching her memory by allowing a new dog to use her things. On the contrary, keeping some of the old things around and in use provides a nice sense of continuity with the home's previous canine inhabitant.

First, you'll need a collar and leash. Actually, you'll need two collars, one a "choke" or "training" collar and the other an everyday or "buckle" collar to which you'll attach the dog's tags. Some dog owners mistakenly leave their dogs in a training collar all the time; this is a prescription for disaster, especially for a rambunctious puppy. This type of collar (which tightens when a ring is pulled) can easily get caught on furniture or shrubbery and strangle the dog. So a buckle collar is the only type of collar to leave on your dog when you're not around.

If you've brought home a Boxer puppy, you'll undoubtedly go through

Training collars are useful for teaching your Boxer not to tug on her leash when you're walking together.

several buckle collars in the first year as your dog grows. In fact, she'll grow so quickly that you need to remember to check her collar at least once a week to make sure it has not suddenly gotten too tight. You should be able to easily slip two fingers between the dog's neck and the collar. If it's tight, move to the next notch on the collar or move on to the next collar size. By the end of the first year, your dog will probably be wearing the collar size she'll wear from then on.

Buckle collars are available in leather, nylon, and cotton web. Nylon is generally the most durable, but the edges can sometimes be sharp, so make sure the collar is something your Boxer can wear comfortably all day, every day. Cotton web collars are softer but won't last as long, and leather collars are expensive. Check them all out and then make your choice. But remember that comfort is especially important for short-haired dogs like Boxers. They don't have a lot of fur between their skin and the collar.

Your puppy probably won't take to her new collar right away. Most likely, she's never worn one before, and it will make a funny jingling sound when she walks. Most dogs soon get used to a collar, though; some even get upset when you take it off. To your dog, her collar will become a part of her.

Make sure that you take a leash and collar along when you pick up your Boxer puppy from the breeder.

"Choke" collars are usually made of chain and metal links. These collars slip over the dog's head for training and walking. The leash almost always attaches to the choke collar. That's because when you're walking or training your Boxer, a buckle collar will not hold her securely. She can slip her head out of it.

As important as any collar is the leash. It's usually made of the same material as the collar—leather, cotton mesh, or nylon. Choose one that feels right in your hand. The crucial thing is that your dog must always be on a leash whenever she leaves the house. No matter how well-trained your Boxer becomes, or how closely she seems to stick by your side, you never know what might happen, and there are more cars and trucks on the roads every day. Even the most disciplined dog sometimes cannot resist the allure of another dog across the street or a bouncing ball in the driveway. It only takes one mistake for you to lose your beloved canine companion.

The standard dog leash is six feet (1.8 meters) long and it has a metal clasp on one end so you can attach your pet's training collar. At the other end is a loop through which you can slip your hand to keep a tight grip. Many owners of larger dogs (and a Boxer, while not the largest, is still a big, powerful dog) also wrap the leash once around their hand for an even more secure grip. This can be helpful in case your Boxer suddenly lunges at another dog. Because of all this hand-wrapping, many Boxer owners prefer cotton webbing or leather leashes to the rough nylon ones.

Another leash option that's increasing in popularity is the retractable leash. This type of leash spools out as your dog moves forward and retracts when you want her back, almost like reeling in a fish. It can also lock at a certain length. A retractable leash can be bulky and a bit heavy, but it's nice to have when you take your dog to a park or to the shore and she wants a little more freedom to romp. Letting her roam on a retractable collar isn't the best option for teaching your Boxer to walk by your side, however. Let her view this as a special treat, and make her regular walks around the neighborhood a more disciplined prance by your side. This will make for a better-behaved Boxer at home.

Another essential for your new canine family member is a crate. Dog crates are usually made of wire or hard plastic, with large air vents or windows on the sides and a door of metal grating that snaps in place. The plastic crates also break down

Crates can be made from plastic or wire; the latter enable your Boxer to more easily see what is going on around her when she's inside. Whichever kind of crate you choose, it should be large enough for your Boxer to stand up, stretch out, and turn around.

into two pieces, with the top fitting into the bottom for convenient storage (though once you put it together, you'll find it so handy that you'll never take it apart). The crate is important for both your puppy and your adult dog. In fact, you may have to buy two crates, if you get your new Boxer as a puppy—one to fit the small dog, and a larger one for her when she's full grown.

The crate has many uses. First, it's a crucial component of your puppy's housetraining routine, especially if you don't expect to be home to take your pup outside every hour. That's because a dog—even a puppy—will not foul her own "den," and therefore will wait until she's

taken out to relieve herself. A crate also comes in handy to keep your puppy safe when doors are being opened or a lot of people are in the house. It can also be a refuge for a puppy that has misbehaved and can't seem to keep from being underfoot at a hectic time. A pup or a "teenage" dog that is kept in a crate while you're away is a dog that will not make mischief while she's unsupervised. Finally, most dogs grow to love their crates. A crate is her "room," her refuge, a place to go when she wants to get away from it all and relax. Many dogs choose to sleep in their crates at night.

Your crate, whether made of plastic or wire mesh, should be large enough so that your dog can stand up, turn around, and lie down in it without being too restricted. A bunch of old towels or a fluffy rug on the bottom will complete the interior design, and your Boxer will be happy as a clam. Her needs and desires are wonderfully simple.

Another puppy item that's not essential but will come in quite handy is a baby gate (or two). These are accordionlike wood or plastic barriers that span a doorway or another open space and keep your puppy confined. They are about three feet (91 cm) tall and will work until your Boxer is old enough not to need them anymore. With a baby gate or two, you can keep your new pup confined to the kitchen, the bathroom, or the laundry room (areas with easy-to-clean tile floors) until she's housebroken.

Last—but certainly not least in your dog's mind—you'll need bowls for food and fresh water and toys to exercise your Boxer's body and

mind. Stainless steel dishes work best because plastic, with regular use, can discolor your pooch's nose, turning it from black to pink. Plastic bowls are also more likely to retain bacteria. Get the types of bowls that come in a raised holder or stand. Otherwise, your Boxer will have to chase them all over the kitchen because they will slide around as she gobbles up her food.

The rule about toys is this: the more the better. Your new pal will need hard, durable chewing toys to work her jaws and teeth, squeaky toys for good old-fashioned fun, balls and disks like Frisbees to chase outdoors, and soft stuffed toys that she'll enjoy carrying when she's feeling mellow.

Now, finally, your home is ready for a Boxer!

Your Boxer should probably be supervised when chewing something that could come apart, like this rawhide bone, as it is possible she might choke on small pieces.

CHAPTER FIVE

Caring for Your Puppy (Birth to Six Months)

Whether you purchase or adopt a puppy, she'll arrive in her new surroundings excited, nervous, and maybe a little scared. Dogs are creatures of habit, and coming home with you for the first time presents a lot of new sensations and challenges. Try to keep things as calm as possible the first few days. This might be difficult if you have children, because they'll want to play with the puppy and hold her. Try to limit this type of contact to a few minutes per child or the pup will become overwhelmed and frightened. If she gets too frightened, she might even nip; that goes for an adult dog, too.

When you first bring the puppy home, have family members all sit on

Playing with your puppy will help her learn that she has nothing to fear in her new home.

the floor in the room where you plan to keep the dog for the first few weeks. That way, your new Boxer can explore her new environment at her own pace, sniffing and checking out each member of the family in her own time. Don't worry, this period of uneasiness won't last long, and your puppy will soon come to view you as her family—her "pack."

The first few nights, your puppy will probably whine. Nights can be as frightening for a dog as they are for a child. You can reduce her nighttime anxiety by fixing her up with a dog bed or a cardboard box with an old cushion, towels, and a cuddly toy inside. Her crate can also be used as a "den." Leave a night-light on, so she can see that there's nothing in the new room to fear, and perhaps even leave a radio on, playing softly. Avoid the temptation to take the new puppy to bed with you. Once established, this sleeping arrangement is hard to break, and a grown-up Boxer can hog a lot of bed space (not to mention stealing the covers and drinking out of your bedside water glass).

CANINE FIRST AID

When a dog joins your family, it's important to have canine first aid supplies on hand. Your canine first aid kit should contain the following items:

- gauze pads
- antibiotic ointment
- hydrogen peroxide
- petroleum jelly
- eye wash
- ear wash
- medications
- bismuth tablets
- sterile stretch gauze
- bandage scissors
- splints
- a blanket
- tweezers
- tensor bandage
- rectal thermometer
- paperwork, including the dog's health record
- medications
- local and national poison control numbers
- phone numbers for your regular veterinary clinic and the emergency clinic.

THE FIRST VISIT TO THE VET

You should make a veterinary appointment within forty-eight hours of bringing your pup home. The tone you set for your pup before and during her first trip to the vet is possibly the most important part of the visit. If her experience is traumatic, she may very well hide under the bed every time you grab the car keys in the future. So keep everything calm and happy. Make going in the car seem like a treat. Most dogs love car trips, as long as they don't associate them with eventual pain and discomfort. Create as many positive reinforcements as you can. A pocket full of dog treats for the journey is a very good start.

On the day of the visit, make sure to take all the papers (including the vaccination schedule) that the breeder gave you. If you adopted your Boxer pup from a shelter, bring any paperwork about your pup that you received from the shelter staff. Also, you'll need to take a fecal sample (a plastic sandwich bag works well) so the vet can check for parasites.

Puppies should begin their vaccinations when they are six to eight

VACCINATION SCHEDULE FOR PUPPIES

The following vaccination schedule is recommended by the American Animal Hospital Association:

Vaccine	Age of Puppy
Distemper	8 weeks and 12 weeks
Parvovirus	8 weeks, 12 weeks, 16 weeks
Parainfluenza	8 weeks, 12 weeks
Coronavirus	8 weeks, 12 weeks
Canine adenovirus-2	8 weeks, 12 weeks
Leptospirosis	8 weeks, 12 weeks
Bordetella*	12 weeks
Lyme disease*	12 weeks, 16 weeks
Rabies +	16 weeks

* Optional vaccines, depending on location and risk.   + Required by law.
Source: American Animal Hospital Association

FAST FACT

Make sure your dog wears her rabies tag at all times. If she ever gets away from you, she's more likely to be rescued if someone sees that she's had her rabies shots.

weeks old. Usually the breeder will have already completed the first vaccination and deworming. (Boxers adopted from shelters may or may not have received any vaccinations.) After this first vet visit, your puppy should be vaccinated every three to four weeks until she's 16 to 20 weeks old. Some vets, being cautious, will also recommend that the pup be dewormed again with each vaccination. The vaccination usually consists of one shot that protects against several diseases: distemper, adenovirus, parvovirus, and parainfluenza. Sometimes vaccines against leptospirosis and coronavirus are also included.

At 16 weeks, your pup can also receive her first rabies shot. You should not overlook this vaccine, because rabies is on the rise in several parts of the United States, and a simple scratch from an infected raccoon in your backyard could be a death sentence for your dog. In addition, state laws require all dog owners to vaccinate their dogs against rabies. After the initial rabies vaccination, the vet will probably recommend yearly rabies booster shots for your dog.

The vet will also give your pup a head-to-toe examination to make sure each of her systems is in good order. He will start at the head,

checking ears, eyes, gums, and teeth for anything out of the ordinary. He will examine the pup's skin for signs of dryness, dandruff, fleas, or ticks. Feeling and pressing on the abdomen (a process known as palpating), the vet will make sure the puppy has no blockages, swollen organs, tenderness, or pain. He will palpate the belly button for an umbilical hernia as well.

With a stethoscope, he will listen to the pup's lungs and heart, trying to detect any heart murmurs, irregular heartbeats, or raspy breathing. He will also check the genitals for abnormal development or unusual discharges.

Finally, your veterinarian will examine your dog's hips for early signs of hip dysplasia. He'll also examine the puppy's knees and elbows, moving them around to see that they're operating smoothly. If you plan to show your Boxer eventually, tell the vet, and he will also check for evenness of bite and other things contest judges seek in a champion.

If your Boxer pup is otherwise healthy, her biggest problem, and your biggest headache, will be parasites. Parasites are a canine's worst enemy, making her uncomfortable at best, and threatening her health at worst.

Your veterinarian will thoroughly examine your Boxer puppy during her first visit.

Fleas and ticks can be difficult to avoid if your Boxer goes outside, and she undoubtedly will. You can try to keep these parasites under control by bathing your dog with a flea shampoo and checking her for fleas and ticks periodically. Boxers are lucky in that their short coat makes it easy for you to detect and remove parasites. (For more on fleas and ticks, see pages 71–73.)

Mosquitoes are another story. They are more than a nuisance, because they often carry a parasite called microfilaria. When a mosquito bites a dog, some microfilaria are injected into the canine's bloodstream. Within about three months, the microfilaria will migrate into the dog's heart and develop into adult worms. Each adult worm can reach a length of 12 inches (30.5 cm) or more. Within six to eight months, these adults begin to reproduce, adding more heartworms to the dog's growing load. If a tangle of these worms clogs a dog's heart, it cannot pump efficiently, so the dog becomes weak and sick. A heavy load of heartworms, left untreated, will bring on the dog's death.

All dogs should be on some type of heartworm preventive, which guards against this life-threatening parasite by killing the microfilaria before they can develop into adult heartworms. Your vet can suggest the best heartworm preventive for your pup.

However, before dogs are given heartworm preventives, they must be tested to make sure they're not already infected. It can be fatal to administer preventive heartworm medication to a dog with adult heartworms. A different regimen is needed to clear up a heartworm infection. Because treating heartworm infection is dangerous, and sometimes fatal, it's much better to prevent infections from occurring.

THE DANGER OF HEARTWORMS

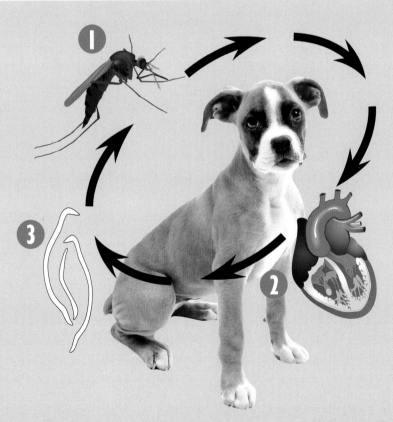

Heartworms are a concern for all dog owners. The graphic above illustrates the cycle of heartworm development. When a mosquito (1) bites a Boxer, it can inject microfilaria into her bloodstream. The microfilaria travel through the bloodstream to the heart (2), where they grow into heartworms (3) and multiply, clogging the dog's heart. If left untreated, heartworms can kill.

PUPPY NUTRITION

Eats! That will soon become your puppy's favorite word, a clarion call that will rouse her from a dead sleep and send her careening down the hall to the kitchen and her food dish. But making sure your pup gets the right food for health and longevity—a food she likes and eats—can be a frustrating, trial-and-error process.

Puppies generally come to their owners already eating solid food, because most of them are weaned from their mother's milk by the age of six weeks. More mature Boxer puppies will have weaned themselves at four or five weeks of age. The timing doesn't matter as much as the food she's eating when you take her home. Rapid changes in diet can upset delicate puppy tummies, so ask the breeder what type of food your puppy was eating and how much. Most responsible breeders will send their puppies off with small bags of their regular food, to help the new owners until they can get to the store to buy their own.

Your puppy's breeder most likely had her on a quality puppy food. You'll want to keep her on puppy food until she's at least 12 months old or even 18 months of age. If she's eating this food well, you're lucky and should keep her on it. However, if your pup is already starting to turn up her nose at the food, you can try to introduce another puppy chow slowly into her diet. Mix new food with her existing food in increasing amounts over the course of a week or so, until you are feeding her only the

ESSENTIAL VITAMINS AND MINERALS

The nutritional needs of dogs are similar to, but not exactly the same as, those of humans. Most experts agree that our canine pals cannot be healthy and happy without the following vitamins: vitamin A, vitamin D, vitamin E, vitamin K, vitamin B_1 (thiamin), riboflavin, vitamin B_6, niacin, pantothenic acid, vitamin B_{12}, and folic acid. Vitamin A is especially important for Boxers to maintain good vision and a healthy immune system.

The following minerals are also essential for your dog: calcium, phosphorous, magnesium, sodium, potassium, chlorine, iron, copper, zinc, manganese, selenium, and iodine.

Don't leave kibble in your puppy's bowl and allow her to pick at the food whenever she's hungry. Instead, leave her food out for about 15 minutes at mealtimes, then take the bowl away until it's time for her next feeding. Your Boxer must have access to fresh water throughout the day, however—especially if the weather is hot or if she's been playing hard.

new food. Special puppy food is necessary for growing pups because it contains the proper ratios of vitamins and minerals they need to handle their growth spurts and rapidly developing systems.

When you pick a puppy food, check the label to be sure it has been certified by the Association of American Feed Control Officials (AAFCO) or the Canadian Veterinary Medical Association (CVMA), if you live in Canada. These two organizations test pet foods to make certain they meet minimum nutritional standards.

Your puppy should be fed three times a day—morning, noon, and evening. Each meal should include just enough food so that she seems satisfied without stuffing herself or leaving any in her bowl. To know if your dog is eating the right amount,

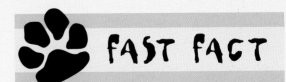

FAST FACT

Puppies (and adult dogs) have fewer taste buds than people. That's why they can eat things that most people think are disgusting.

press her side with the flat of your hand. If you can just barely feel her ribs, you're probably feeding her properly. If her ribs are prominent, she's not eating enough. If you can't feel her ribs at all, you've got a little porker on your hands and you need to cut back on the food.

MAKING YOUR PUP A WELL-BEHAVED FAMILY MEMBER

One of the most important things your new Boxer puppy needs to learn is how to be a welcome addition to the family. Even though dogs and humans have been hanging out together for centuries, every puppy still needs to be taught the ground rules for successfully living with a family. To accomplish this, family members must all work together. Basic commands, like "come," "sit," and "down," must be uniform and practiced continually (more about basic puppy training later). Everyone in the household should also lavish praise on your pup when she does what she's told. Treats like dog biscuits are also quite effective in getting your new puppy to cooperate.

Much of a puppy's early socialization comes from her mother. That's why it's best if puppies remain with their mothers until they're at least eight weeks old. Their mothers are amazing teachers, instructing the young pups that it's not acceptable to play too roughly or bite too hard. After eight weeks, it's up to their masters to continue these lessons.

When you bring your new puppy home, it's understandable that you'll be a little overprotective, at least at first. After all, your puppy's health and safety are your responsibility. But overprotectiveness is not the best thing for your dog. The period from eight to twelve weeks is especially crucial for socialization. During this time, you should

Socialize your Boxer by taking him on walks through your neighborhood and letting him meet other people and animals.

SAFE SOCIALIZING

When you begin to socialize your Boxer puppy, remember that she still has an immature immune system and is very susceptible to disease, especially before she's received all of her vaccinations. This does not mean you must keep your puppy locked in the house. It just means that, during the first few months, you must take precautions when you take her outside or have people over.

Numerous parasites and diseases are carried around on the bottoms of shoes, so when you come home or when other people come into your home, shoes should be taken off at the door. (You may want to hide the shoes, as your Boxer may want to chew on them!) Also, you and your guests should always wash your hands before handling the puppy.

When you are out walking with your Boxer puppy, you will undoubtedly come across other dog owners doing the very same thing. Although it's good to introduce your Boxer to other dogs in the neighborhood, they may be carrying parasites or diseases that can cause your little pup severe problems. It's best to avoid the canine greeting ritual until your puppy has received all of her vaccines or your veterinarian says it's okay.

introduce your Boxer pup to as many new people and situations as you safely can. Have family and friends over to get to know the new puppy. Walk her, on a leash, all around the neighborhood and allow her to exercise her innate curiosity by checking out different sights and smells. Take her for rides in the car, provided you won't be away from the vehicle for more than a few minutes at a time. All these experiences will establish self-confidence and reinforce proper behavior under new and unusual circumstances. This is especially important if you plan to enter your Boxer in shows or Obedience competitions.

In the eight-week-old to twelve-week-old period, your puppy is experiencing some major lifestyle changes. Just imagine: she has gone from nursing to solid food, has been separated from her mother and littermates, and has been introduced to a whole new set of people who are constantly telling her what to do. Except she can't understand them. Try to keep new experiences during this period as upbeat and positive as possible for your pup, because this is also known as the fear-imprint

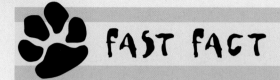

FAST FACT

Your puppy will occasionally seem to go nuts and race around the house, over furniture, and under tables and chairs. It will be impossible to stop her. This is natural. You should just let her wear herself out.

period. Anything frightening or unpleasant that happens to the dog during this period of major adjustment can have a lasting impact on her behavior. If she's made to feel insecure, she may remain insecure for the rest of her life.

Remember, too, that during the first year of your dog's life she's going through many physical and mental changes. Some researchers believe that a canine's fear periods are triggered by nutritional deficiencies caused by growth spurts. That's why it's important for your puppy to get a proper diet. But when these fear periods occur, and your pup seems especially unnerved by something relatively inconsequential, don't overreact or coddle her. This will reinforce in her mind that what she fears is worth fearing. Instead, you can react in one of two ways. Both are effective. Either praise and pet her playfully, as if nothing at all

is frightening, or ignore her fearfulness completely. Eventually, she'll realize that what she initially feared is not all that terrifying after all.

The bottom line is that the earlier your Boxer pup is introduced to a variety of people, surroundings, and other animals, the happier both you and your Boxer will be.

SEPARATION ANXIETY

Most dogs will feel anxious when you leave them home alone. They are, after all, pack animals, and you're now their pack. As the comedian Jake Johanson jokingly says, dogs left alone panic because they don't know how the appliances work. But a canine with serious separation anxiety is no laughing matter. She may bark nonstop, scratch and claw at a door, or race around the house destroying things. She may even urinate or defecate in her crate out of nervousness.

Canine separation anxiety can be reduced or eliminated if everyone in the family works together. That means that when any of you leave the house, it's far better not to make a big deal out of it. If you mug with your Boxer and tell her how much you're going to miss her, she'll think that your leaving is a serious issue, maybe even something long-term to justify such a fuss. Likewise, it's best not to tell the dog that she's in charge while you're gone and to make sure no one breaks in. While, of course, your Boxer can't understand the words you're saying, she can intuit quite a bit from your tone of voice and body language. When you leave your Boxer home alone, it's better to simply slip out without fanfare.

GROOMING YOUR BOXER PUPPY

Boxers are a short-coated breed and thus don't need a lot of grooming to look their best. Still, there are some grooming basics that every Boxer owner should perform to keep his Boxer healthy and feeling good. In addition to brushing, these grooming essentials include checking for fleas and ticks and removing any you find, keeping teeth and gums clean and plaque-free, trimming toenails, and checking ears periodically and removing any debris. Boxers

Regular brushing will help your Boxer look her best, by removing dirt and loose hair while spreading natural oils throughout her coat. For best results, use a bristle brush.

are easier to groom than many other breeds, so there's no reason you can't do this yourself at home. Grooming your own Boxer is an excellent way for the two of you to continue bonding. Plus, it gives you an opportunity to thoroughly examine your Boxer. You'll soon get to know the lumps and bumps on her body, so that when you're grooming her you can spot any abnormal growths and get them checked out quickly by your veterinarian. But if you simply don't have the time to devote to your Boxer's grooming, it's far better to take her to a professional groomer than to not groom her at all.

BRUSHING: If you're finicky about loose dog hair in your house, you might want to escort your Boxer outside to brush her. This way all the dirt, dander, and hair will not end up as little tumbleweeds in the corners of your living room. Most dogs will enjoy the brushing experience if it's done properly. That means brushing with long strokes, using mild to moderate pressure. If your Boxer starts to squirm, then you're brushing too hard. Also, it's important to get the proper brush for a short-haired dog. No big wire bristles for a Boxer! A softer, natural-bristle brush or a glove-brush should be all you need.

Your brushing technique should resemble a massage. Start at the base of the head and brush toward the tail, removing any hair or debris that collects in the brush. Then brush down each leg. When you've finished, your Boxer's coat will shine.

BATHING: Once a month is often enough to bathe a short-haired dog like the Boxer. If it's warm outside, a bath can be done out of doors. But remember that water from a garden hose is cold, and you want your best friend's bath to be refreshing, not freezing. If the bath becomes an unpleasant experience, your Boxer will make future baths very difficult for both of you. She may even decide that you could use a bath, too.

Many vets recommend using a shampoo especially formulated for dogs, but unless your Boxer has a problem with parasites (thus requiring a special shampoo), plain old baby shampoo should also work fine. It's mild enough not to irritate your Boxer's skin.

To begin, get your dog completely wet. Then squeeze a line of shampoo along her backbone, and put a little more on her chest. This should be enough to lather up her whole body. Be careful not to get soap in her eyes or water in her ears. Placing cotton balls in her ears before you begin the bath will help keep water from getting into them. Also, it's a good idea to wait until you've washed your Boxer's body before you try to wash her head. Once your dog's head gets wet, she will want to shake herself dry—and she'll probably soak you in the process.

A Boxer whose ears have been cropped is less likely to develop ear infections than a Boxer whose ears are left natural. However, all Boxers need to have their ears cleaned on a regular basis.

After you've rinsed the shampoo from your Boxer's coat, gently remove the cotton balls from her ears to check for waxy buildup, mites, or signs of infection. If you spot any of these things, clean them out with a dry or slightly moist cloth. If your Boxer's ears have been left long (uncropped), they will be more susceptible to infection, especially if you live in a warm climate and her ears tend to get wet. You'll know infected dog ears when you encounter them because they smell foul. If you encounter a problem inside your dog's ears that you cannot clear up at home or that seems to be getting worse, a trip to the vet is definitely in order. You can help make sure that doesn't happen by keeping your dog's ears clean and free of hair. Just snip any stray hairs you see inside her ears every few weeks.

NAIL CARE: Trimming your Boxer's toenails will likely be her least favorite part of the grooming experience. Still, unless your dog walks several miles a day on a hard, rough surface like asphalt, trimming will be necessary.

It's absolutely essential for you to get a special dog-nail trimmer for this job. Don't even attempt to perform the task with scissors or

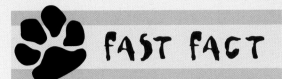

FAST FACT

When clipping your Boxer's toenails, you'll occasionally clip the quick (as hard as you try not to) and it will bleed. So before you start, make sure you have some form of quick-stop powder—like styptic powder—handy to put on the bleeding nail.

shears of any type. The Boxer's nails are too hard, and she may jerk away, thus getting cut. You can find these special clippers in any pet supply store. Look for the type that resembles a miniature guillotine, and purchase the large size, because a Boxer's feet grow big.

Stand behind the dog for this job, lifting each front foot and gently bending it backwards at the knee. Now look for the quick. The quick is the dark blood vessel that nourishes the nail. You do not want to clip this! It will bleed, your dog will holler, and she'll hate having her nails done. The quick usually stops about a quarter of an inch (6 mm) from the end of the nail. Once you've found it, put the clipper over the nail and squeeze the handle. The tip of the nail will pop off. If you're in doubt about the location of the quick, just clip off tiny portions of the nail until you see it. Nails on the back feet are done the same way.

DENTAL CARE: Finally, there is your Boxer's dental hygiene (for that winning Boxer smile!). The good news is that you don't have to brush her teeth after every meal, but you should do this at least once a week. That will help keep tartar and plaque from building up. You can use a regular toothbrush or a finger brush, but make sure to use a toothpaste specially formulated for dogs. Your Boxer won't appreciate the minty flavor of human toothpaste, and the chemicals in it can be harmful to her health. If any discoloring on your dog's teeth cannot be removed with a brush, you'll have to take her to the vet for a tooth cleaning.

HOUSETRAINING YOUR BOXER PUP

The most basic training for a new puppy is housetraining. There are

Housetraining can be frustrating, but be patient. With proper training, your Boxer will soon learn that she must only eliminate her urine or feces outside.

several schools of thought on how to do this most effectively, but this section will deal with the housebreaking technique that most trainers endorse.

For this you'll need a crate (which you should purchase before you bring your puppy home). Dogs, even puppies, will generally not eliminate in their crates. This is where your puppy will be put when you leave the house for any length of time. If you're going to be out for more than a few hours, someone else will need to come in to let your puppy relieve herself outdoors.

But while you're home, you'll need to work diligently to establish in your puppy's mind that outside is the only acceptable place to urinate or defecate. Naturally, it will take a little while for this notion to sink in, even for an intelligent dog like a Boxer, but if you're gentle and consistent, you'll be amazed at how quickly your dog will learn.

A good rule of thumb is that puppies have to eliminate every hour or two. In addition, they'll need to go right after they wake up and right after they come out of their crates. They'll also need to go about fifteen minutes after eating or drinking.

While you're around, try as hard as possible to take your puppy outside on a leash once an hour. Take her to the same spot in the yard each

time you go out, and encourage her to eliminate using a phrase like "go potty" or "do business." Whenever she eliminates outdoors, be lavish

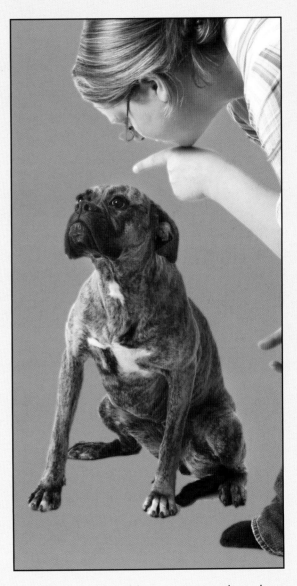

It won't help to scold your puppy when she has an accident, and never rub her nose in the mess. Just take her to the designated place for elimination, and praise her lavishly when she does what you want.

Remember, a well-exercised puppy is often a well-behaved puppy.

with your praise. Pat her head, pet her, and make her feel as if she's just done the greatest thing in the world. Conversely, if she has an accident indoors (and she will), don't punish her for this indiscretion. Never rub her nose in the mess, hit her, or yell at her—she won't understand, and the only lesson she'll learn is that you're mean and not to be trusted. Instead, immediately pick her up and take her outside. Eventually, she'll come to associate her feelings of relief with the great outdoors.

It's that simple. Some dogs take longer to housebreak than others, but if you follow these steps consistently, your Boxer pup should be mostly housebroken within several weeks. However, it may take six months to a year before she is fully housetrained.

CREATING A POLITE PET

Beyond not eliminating in the house, there will be other household rules you'll have to teach your dog to make her pleasant company for you and anyone else who might happen to drop by. What these rules will be is up to you, but generally they'll include not begging for food at the dining table, not jumping on family members or guests to greet them, not barking incessantly and disturbing the neighbors, not jumping on the furniture, and not fighting or chasing other pets in the family (outside of an occasional game of "chase me.")

Again, as with housebreaking, consistency is the key. When you see the dog misbehaving, gently but firmly correct her by removing her (say, from the new sofa) and then making her sit. Do the same thing every time, because if you let a dog get away with bad behavior just one time, it will be much harder to correct her the next time. (A method for teaching your Boxer the basic obedience commands is found in Chapter Six.)

All members of the family must make sure your Boxer abides by the rules. Kids like to sneak food to the family dog under the table, so it's important to stress to them that they, too, are responsible for creating a polite pet.

Your "Teenage" Boxer (Six Months to Two Years)

Like it or not, when your Boxer is between the ages of six months and two years, you have a canine "teenager" on your hands. And like a human teen, your Boxer will try your patience at times. Starting at about the age of eight months, your Boxer will experience a surge of hormones; these will be accompanied by behavior changes. She'll still have the energy level and playfulness of a puppy, racing around the house like a lunatic, but by the time she's two she'll be fully grown, weighing 40 to

As your Boxer grows larger physically, her personality will also develop and mature.

50 pounds (18 to 23 kg). Keep in mind, too, that much of this weight is solid Boxer muscle.

Like a human teen, your Boxer will start to rebel during this time. She may question your authority, or seem to go deaf when you issue commands. She won't sit when you say, "Sit," or come when you call her. Don't let her get away with this behavior, or she'll think she can take your position as head of the pack. Keep up with the basic commands that she should be starting to learn ("come," "sit," "down," and "stay," which will be discussed later in this chapter) and throw in a couple of new ones just to remind her who's boss. Firmly but kindly insist that she obey you—the first time you issue a command.

This trying time will pass, of course. When it does, be sure you're still in command.

HEALTH ISSUES

By now your Boxer should have received her initial vaccinations for distemper, hepatitis, leptospirosis, parvovirus, parainfluenza, and rabies. Your vet may also recommend that your dog be immunized against bordetella (kennel cough), coronavirus, and/or Lyme disease. So the bulk of her initial immunizations are behind her, although she will require

some boosters. Your veterinarian will provide the schedule for these shots.

Health issues for the "teen" Boxer should be minimal. Still, there are matters like parasite control that you'll have to address. When your Boxer goes outside, for instance, she's almost guaranteed to come back in with a few unwanted guests: fleas and ticks.

FLEAS: The most common and irritating of canine parasites are fleas. Once your Boxer picks up fleas, you must wage an all-out war on them in your house. Each adult flea can lay 20 to 30 batches of eggs, and most of these eggs will fall off your dog inside your house. There, within several days to several months, they will hatch and hitch a ride on your Boxer. (Fleas aren't choosy. If you look tasty, they may hop on you, too.) If you haven't

Fleas can not only cause your Boxer's skin to become irritated, they also transmit parasitic diseases such as tapeworms.

started your counterattack, you'll soon have a serious flea infestation on your hands.

The first step is to bathe your dog with a veterinarian-recommended flea shampoo. Follow the directions carefully so that it will be effective. Luckily for both of you, your Boxer's short coat, especially when wet, will make it difficult for fleas to hide. They can then be washed away. Next, while your dog is drying in a room with the door closed, thoroughly vacuum the rest of the house, paying special attention to the carpets and baseboards, where fleas like to hide. Then vacuum the room the dog was in. Unfortunately, you'll have to repeat this whole-house vacuuming routine every day for several weeks. And each time, be sure to empty the vacuum outside, and put the contents in a sealed garbage bag. If the problem inside your house seems especially stubborn, pick up some insect growth regulator (IGR) from a pet supply store and apply it around the house according to the directions on the package.

It may be tempting, but don't be too quick to reach for the flea collars, sprays, or insecticides. While effective at killing insects, these toxic substances can also be quite harmful to both your Boxer and your family. With regular flea baths and daily vacuuming, you should be able to keep any flea problem under control.

TICKS: Another parasite your dog might encounter is the tick. Ticks are usually found in grassy or wooded areas and will cling to your dog as she brushes up against them. If you and your Boxer enjoy a romp in the woods, make sure to check her coat thoroughly when you get back home. Wood ticks are easy to spot (they're small, dark, crablike creatures) and are slow moving, so they can be removed from the body with tweezers. Deer ticks are smaller and lighter in color, but they're more dangerous than wood ticks because they carry Lyme disease.

If you find a tick on your dog, it should be removed as quickly as possible by grasping the tick close to the

Every time your Boxer plays outside, check her carefully for ticks. If you find one, it should be removed immediately.

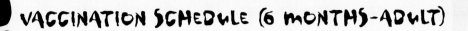

VACCINATION SCHEDULE (6 MONTHS-ADULT)

The following vaccination schedule is recommended by the American Animal Hospital Association:

Vaccine	Age for Boosters
Distemper	1 year, then every 3 years
Parvovirus	1 year, then every 3 years
Parainfluenza	1 year, then every 3 years
Coronavirus	1 year, then every 3 years
Canine adenovirus-2	1 year, then every 3 years
Leptospirosis	1 year, then every 3 years
Bordetella *	1 year, then as needed
Lyme disease *	1 year, then prior to tick season
Rabies +	1 year, then every 3 years

* Optional vaccines, depending on location and risk.

\+ Required by law. Some states still require annual boosters.

Source: American Animal Hospital Association

head with tweezers, then pulling it off. The longer a tick remains embedded in your dog's skin, the greater the chance it will transmit a tick-borne disease to your dog!

Should you get a tick infestation in your house, use the same methods you used to get rid of fleas.

STAYING IN SHAPE

The Boxer is an athlete. One look at the muscles that ripple under her taut coat will confirm that. So she needs a good amount of exercise every day to stay healthy, mentally sharp, happy, and well-behaved.

Since there are few things more enjoyable than a long walk with a canine companion, everyone in the family should be urged to exercise right along with the dog. If, for physical or scheduling reasons, you can't do this, you can join your dog in the backyard after work for a rousing session of ball-chasing or Frisbee. This, too, should be done every day, if possible. You'll probably find that you look forward to it, and nothing will make your Boxer happier. She'll let you know when she's had enough. Remember, a tired Boxer is a Boxer that won't be looking for mischief.

NUTRITION

By the age of one year, your Boxer should be weaned from high-protein puppy food. In fact, there is a school of thought now that dogs prone to hip dysplasia (Boxers, Retrievers, German Shepherds) should be started on adult dog food at six months or even three months. Why? Because some researchers believe that the additional protein and calcium in puppy food, which promotes healthy bone growth in young puppies, actually increases the older dog's chances of developing the debilitating disease. Talk to your vet if you're concerned about this issue.

Boxers, though they're sturdy on the outside, are constitutionally one of the more fragile breeds. This just means that your Boxer will stay healthier longer if you feed her good food. When you shop for dog food, stay away from the cheapest brands. They are formulated with the worst-quality meats (you don't even want to know what's in them) and are usually chock full of preservatives. Try to find a dog food made with human-grade ingredients and without a lot of artificial preservatives. Read the package labels to make the wisest choice.

Until she was about six months old, your Boxer probably ate three meals a day. Now it's time to cut down to two meals, a morning and an evening feeding. Never give your Boxer a big pile of food at once and expect it to last all day. Boxers are prone to bloat, a life-threatening disorder in which the dog's stomach fills with gas (see page 85–86), so it's best not to give them meals that are too large.

Where you feed your Boxer is up to you, but a quiet spot where she can enjoy her food uninterrupted and not make a mess will work out best for everyone. A corner of the kitchen, say, or inside her crate, is ideal. Make sure your Boxer knows that you're the boss when it comes to her food. She should have to sit politely and wait for you to set her bowl down and tell her she can proceed. This will get her started eating calmly (again reducing the likelihood of bloat), and keep her from jumping at the food as you're trying to prepare it.

SOCIALIZATION

If you did your homework, you took your brand-new puppy almost everywhere and introduced her to a bunch of new people, places, and situations—all safe and nonthreatening, of course. By the time she is six months old, your dog will have started to develop a degree of self-confidence in interacting with the larger world, so you don't want there to be any unexpected setbacks. Keep her new encounters nonthreatening, and make sure you control them. On your morning walks, don't introduce your dog to an unfamiliar dog, because you don't know if that dog will be aggressively defending his owner or his turf. Instead, let the dogs be your guide. If they express a willingness to meet, then let them meet, but keep the exchange brief.

Likewise, you can introduce your budding adult dog to neighbors and new streets with new sights. Remember, your dog takes her cues from you. If you seem nervous or hostile, she'll pick up on your discomfort. Stay calm and confident, and your dog will feel that she has nothing to fear when she's with you.

It's also important for you to let your dog explore a little when she walks with you. Let her sniff those interesting places; she's taking in a

Your Boxer must be properly socialized so that she plays well with other dogs, rather than becoming aggressive.

world of information about her sur-roundings. When you've had enough, simply tug the leash and say, "Let's go." Needless to say, never let your Boxer sniff another animal's feces or any food you might find. That's where nasty diseases reside.

BASIC COMMANDS

Because your Boxer's "teen" period will be the time she decides to rebel and pretend that you've never taught her anything, now would be a good time to review her basic training. Teaching a dog to do certain things on command is not bossy or cruel. On the contrary, a dog under her owner's control is a safe dog. Besides, dogs don't dislike commands. Like a child, they need limits; they need to know where they stand.

The first thing you'll want to do is get your dog to come when you call her. She'll already be familiar with her name, so use it as often as possi-ble when you're talking to her. First, put your dog in a sitting position, facing you. Walk several steps away. Then, as invitingly as you can, say her name and follow it with the com-mand, "Come!" For example, "Zoey, come!" With your voice, make her want to come, and when she does, make it worth her while. Reward her with lavish praise and a treat. Treats

are helpful for the first few sessions, but should not be continued forever. Tell her what a good girl she is.

Now you should incorporate the "sit" command at the end of "come." After you've praised her for coming, say, "Sit," and push her hindquarters

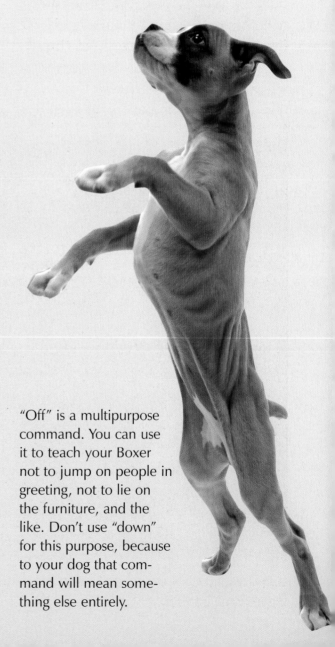

"Off" is a multipurpose command. You can use it to teach your Boxer not to jump on people in greeting, not to lie on the furniture, and the like. Don't use "down" for this purpose, because to your dog that com-mand will mean some-thing else entirely.

into a sitting position. Praise her again. Walk a few steps away and repeat the process.

Remember to say the commands just once, and then make the dog comply. The dog will think you're wishy-washy if you keep repeating a command until she decides to obey you. At this point you're trying to get her to associate "Come" with "Sit," so that every time she comes to you she knows to sit down.

Once your Boxer has mastered "come" and "sit," you're ready to work on two more commands, "down" and "stay." The "down" command begins by getting your Boxer into a sitting position. Push on her shoulder blades until she lies down, while at the same time saying, "Down." Be sure to praise her again when she's in position. Eventually she'll associate the command with the action, and will go down on her own.

With proper training, your Boxer will stay in a sitting position until you release her, no matter what interesting distractions she may see.

BOXER PUSH-UPS

A stubborn adolescent Boxer can be brought around quickly by making her do calisthenics, specifically "push-ups." Face your Boxer, look her in the eyes, and firmly tell her, "Sit." Then tell her "Down." Get her up and repeat the process: sit, down, up; sit, down, up. If she's rebelling to the point that she refuses to sit on command, put your hand firmly on the top of her rump and push her into the sitting position. Do the same thing to get her into the down position, if need be. If you do this 15 to 20 times whenever your Boxer seems to be rebelling against you and defying your discipline, it can work very well to remind her who is the dog and who is the master.

The "stay" command will be the hardest for your pup to pick up because she'll want to follow you. After all, she gets treats and praise from you! When she's in a sitting or down position, place the palm of your hand in front of her muzzle and say, "Stay." Walk a few steps away, then turn and give the command, "Come." If she stayed until this point, give her praise and a treat, then start the process all over again.

You can try all four basic commands in one session, or you can stick to just "come" and "sit" for a while if your dog seems overwhelmed at first. These are the foundations of basic training, however, so every dog should master them. Don't wear the dog out, though. A training session of ten minutes or so several times a day will suffice at this point in your young Boxer's life.

TRAVELING WITH YOUR BOXER

Eventually, you and your Boxer will have to travel together. Maybe you take a lot of vacations and want to bring your canine companion along, or perhaps you'll have to move across country for work. Either way, you'll have to make special arrangements to travel safely with a dog.

TRAVELING BY CAR: Most of the travel you do with your Boxer will probably be by car. Therefore, get

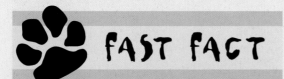

FAST FACT

Most trainers agree that Boxers are among the easiest breeds to train.

her used to riding in an automobile as early as possible. Take her for rides around the neighborhood or to the park. That way, she'll come to associate pleasant things with travel and will want to join you. Depending on how comfortable you are with dog hair and how calm a traveler your Boxer is, you can have her ride in a crate (she will not be too pleased with this option) or you can allow her to ride in the back (of a hatch-back vehicle or an SUV) or on the seat next to you. If you let her ride uncrated, always secure your Boxer in a harness that attaches to a seat belt to ensure her safety in case of an accident.

For long car trips or highway travel, you should use a crate just to be on the safe side.

TRAVEL BY PLANE: Air travel with your Boxer is more problematic. Hopefully, this will be a rare occurrence, because it's not a pleasant experience for your dog. Because of her size, she'll probably be riding in

Your Boxer will enjoy going on trips with you. However, for her safety always make sure she's strapped into a seat or in a travel crate, as you don't want her roaming loose in the car while you're trying to concentrate on driving.

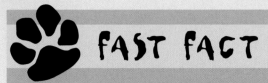

FAST FACT

If you must fly with your dog, try to schedule a direct, nonstop flight. Most pet mishaps occur while changing planes.

the baggage compartment. But if travel by air is unavoidable, there are several steps you can take to make the experience less harrowing for your dog. First, call the airline and get a detailed explanation of what you'll be required to do. Most airlines will make you use their crates for your dog, even if you have your own (make sure theirs is the proper size for your Boxer). Also, you'll have to go to a different part of the terminal—not the regular baggage check-in—to check in with your dog.

Your dog will be nervous throughout the experience, but don't sedate her before boarding. Drugs will only make her feel more disoriented, and, combined with high altitude, could even cause a heart attack. Also, it will be cold in the baggage compartment (but not freezing), so bring along a blanket or rug for her to curl up on. Put in an article of your clothing, too—your scent nearby will reassure her. Make sure she has relieved herself as close to takeoff as possible, and unless it's a long

trip, don't include food and water in the crate. They will likely spill midflight, and then your dog will have to lie in the mess.

Regardless of how you travel with your pet—by land or by air—make sure beforehand that all her immunizations are up-to-date and that her rabies tag and identification tags are secure and legible.

LEAVING YOUR BOXER WITH SOMEONE ELSE

If you have to travel but can't take your Boxer, consider leaving your dog with a boarding kennel or a pet sitter. In many ways, this is a more hassle-free option than bringing her with you. You can leave on vacation or business knowing that your dog will be in good hands.

Many veterinary clinics also have boarding facilities on the premises. This can be a good choice because you already know the vet and the veterinary technicians, and they

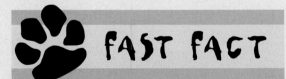

FAST FACT

When boarding your Boxer, look for a kennel that screens the dogs for infectious diseases and parasites. Otherwise, you could bring home a sick, flea-infested dog.

know your dog. They will also be able to handle any medical emergency that might arise with your Boxer. Keep in mind, though, that these will likely be no-frills accommodations. Your dog will spend most of her time in a crate or cage, and will probably be alone at night. Still, this is not a bad option if you'll only be away for a few days.

Caregivers at an independent boarding kennel may also suit your Boxer. These kennels are generally larger facilities, with room for your dog to run and play. But before you choose any kennel, check to make sure it's certified by the American Boarding Kennel Association

(ABKA). Plus, pay a visit and look the kennel over carefully. Make sure it's clean and that other dogs seem to be well treated.

Still another option if you decide to leave your Boxer at home is a pet sitter. This usually costs more than a kennel, but it will be the least disruptive situation for your dog. Dog sitters generally come to your home and either stay there until you get back, or drop in several times a day to feed, water, and walk your dog. Ask your dog-owning friends and neighbors if they can recommend a sitter. Almost every pet owner knows of a sitter who's worth his weight in gold.

CHAPTER SEVEN

Caring for Your Adult Boxer

At two years old, your Boxer is fully mature, and with preventive veterinary care, plenty of exercise, good food, and lots of love from her family, these next few years should be the healthy, happy prime of her life.

If you wish, you can schedule yearly checkups with your vet, but it's also good to keep tabs on your dog's health at home. This can help prevent serious problems later on. Here's what to look for:

COAT: Your Boxer's coat should be clean and shiny. The fur should be thick, not patchy.

SKIN: Her skin should be supple and free of sores or reddish patches.

EARS: Her ears should be free of debris and have no odor.

Your adult Boxer will enjoy sharing just about any outdoor activity with you.

EYES: The eyes should be alert, clear, and clean.

TEETH: Your Boxer's teeth should be white, without traces of yellow or brown.

NAILS: Nails should be even and short enough so they don't curl.

Beyond these concerns, just pay attention to your dog's disposition. You know her better than anyone else, and when she's out of sorts, there's probably a reason. Lethargy and loss of appetite are symptoms of every major canine illness, so if your Boxer shows either, it's time to make a veterinary appointment.

WHEN HEALTH PROBLEMS DO ARISE

Like most dogs, Boxers have their share of breed-specific health concerns. As with any dog diseases, however, potential Boxer problems can be greatly reduced by choosing a reputable, responsible breeder. Unfortunately, though, as the Boxer becomes more and more popular as a breed, more and more backyard breeders will pop up who are just in it for the money. Their dogs will not be as carefully screened for diseases. If you adopted your Boxer from a shelter or a rescue organization, just be on the lookout for signs or

If your dog seems sick or listless for an extended period of time, a visit to your veterinarian may be warranted.

symptoms of these diseases so you can catch them as early as possible.

Let's take a look at common health problems of the Boxer, starting with the most serious ones.

CANCER: Cancer is one of the greatest killers of Boxers, both young and old. In fact, Boxers are one of the top five breeds most prone to this deadly disease. No one knows exactly why Boxers are so susceptible to cancer, but some scientists think the reason may be genetic. That's another reason it's important to know your puppy's family health history, if at all possible. Cancer can also be environmental in origin, so just as you would

with any living thing, you should reduce or eliminate your Boxer's exposure to pesticides and other toxic chemicals. Treatment of this disease in dogs is expensive and, unfortunately, rarely successful.

HEART DISEASE: Heart disease, the second leading killer of Boxers, also has a hereditary origin. Good breeders will seek to reduce the chances of their puppies developing this disease by selective breeding. Still, your Boxer runs a slight risk of developing one of the two types of heart disease most common in this breed.

The first is cardiomyopathy, which involves an abnormal heart

FIT AND TRIM

It is estimated that 25 to 44 percent of dogs in the United States are obese. A Boxer who is carrying extra pounds has a higher risk of developing health problems, so observe these feeding practices to keep your dog trim and healthy:

- Feed your dog a high-quality dog food.

- Measure your dog's food.

- Monitor your dog's weight and adjust the amount you feed him accordingly.

- Feed your dog twice a day on a regular schedule.

- Remove any uneaten food after 20 minutes.

- Avoid enhancing your dog's meal with people food.

- Limit treats and edible chew products.

If you purchased your Boxer from a reputable breeder, both your dog and her parents should have been screened for hereditary conditions. This does not mean, however, that your dog can't develop a heart condition, cancer, or another hereditary disease.

rhythm. Most of the time, this disease is undetectable, even with a thorough exam by your veterinarian. Some dogs with this condition will suddenly die of a heart attack. Others may show warning signs of heart trouble by fainting or seeming overly fatigued. Unfortunately, even if a diagnosis is made, there's not much that can be done for a Boxer suffering cardiomyopathy.

The other heart disease to which Boxers are prone is called aortic stenosis, and this involves a blockage of the aortic valve. Weakness and fainting are also symptoms of this disease, and like cardiomyopathy, there is little that can be done for the dog who has aortic stenosis.

BLOAT: A common problem among Boxers and other barrel-chested breeds like bulldogs, bloat occurs when a dog's stomach fills with gas, swells, and becomes distended. This occurs when a dog gulps air while swallowing food or water, and it can also occur when a Boxer gulps air alone, after vigorous exercise for instance. The bloated stomach impinging on internal organs restricts their function and creates a painful and terrifying situation for the dog. Even more serious, bloat may develop into a life-threatening condition known as torsion, in which the stomach twists and nothing can get into or out of it. The blood builds up carbon dioxide because the inner abdominal pressure prevents the heart and lungs from doing their jobs of cleansing and oxygenating the blood. The dog's blood pressure drops, her body becomes toxic, and the stomach continues to become painfully distended. If this occurs, you must seek immediate veterinary care, as bloat and torsion can kill your Boxer in less than an hour.

Symptoms of bloat include unsuccessful attempts to vomit, increased anxiety and restlessness, and a swollen abdomen that may feel tight like a drum. Your Boxer will probably not act like herself, and may curl into a ball and whine or lick her stomach because she is uncomfortable.

To avoid bloat in your Boxer, give her two small meals each day, rather than one large meal. This will keep her from wolfing down her food out of hunger. Another helpful technique is to soak your dog's kibble in water for five minutes before you feed it to her; this causes the kibble to expand outside of her stomach, rather than inside. In addition, always keep your

Boxer's water bowl full. You don't want her to become so thirsty that she feels compelled to gulp down the water when her bowl is finally filled.

HEATSTROKE: Boxers and other stout, short-nosed dogs were bred to grasp large prey and hang on until their masters arrived. For this purpose, a short nose and a thick muzzle came in quite handy. However, these physical characteristics make it difficult for the Boxer to cool herself by panting. Add to that the Boxer's boundless energy and desire to play all day, and you have a prescription for disaster in hot weather.

Simply put, Boxers are not hot weather dogs. Does this mean that if you live in Florida or Arizona you cannot own a Boxer? Of course not. It just means that during the hottest part of the day, your Boxer should be curled up at your feet in an air-conditioned room instead of left in the backyard.

Heatstroke can come on suddenly, so in warm weather be on the lookout for symptoms. Signs of impending heatstroke include rapid panting, sudden fatigue, and a body temperature above 105° Fahrenheit (40.5° Celsius). Your Boxer may also have a purple tongue and gums and seem confused or disoriented. She will likely also be dehydrated. Should you

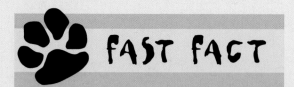

FAST FACT

Boxers don't like weather extremes, either too hot or too cold.

Dogs do not sweat like humans do, so on hot summer days a Boxer must pant and drink water to reduce her core body temperature. A dog that is not able to cool herself is at risk of developing heatstroke, which can be fatal.

notice any of these symptoms, work fast. Get your dog in the shade and wet her down with cool (not icy) water. Then get her to the vet as quickly as possible. Heatstroke can be fatal if not treated immediately, so take precautions when it's hot outside.

NUTRITION FOR YOUR ADULT BOXER

By now, your Boxer's diet has been pretty firmly established. She should be eating reasonable portions of good-quality dog food, with few or no preservatives, twice a day. At this point, you'll want to make sure that she doesn't get fat, so give her a daily dose of exercise. If you're like most dog owners, you enjoy slipping your pal a treat now and then. That's fine, as long as you don't go overboard. Raw bones with the marrow inside are cheap at most grocery stores and are a delightful treat for your Boxer, one that will keep her occupied all day. Put the extra bones in the freezer and pull one out for her if you're going away for the day. However, be sure that any bones you

As a special treat, your Boxer will enjoy chewing a sturdy bone.

get for your Boxer are not the splintering kind. Never give your dog poultry or fish bones, since these easily break apart and could choke her or cause internal damage.

EXERCISE

Remember that Boxers are smart as well as physical. They love games that work their brains and their bodies, and they love to have fun with you. You don't have to be an Olympic athlete to exercise with your Boxer. A Boxer will be in heaven just walking a mile or so with you in the morning or evening.

Likewise, a tennis ball can keep your dog busy for hours, chasing it and returning it to you. Boxers are also known to enjoy pushing around larger balls, such as soccer balls and basketballs. A Frisbee, too, will delight a Boxer, but it's best not to throw it so high that she has to leap up to catch it. Remember that Boxers are prone to hip problems, and too many jarring landings can cause injuries.

A fenced-in yard or a dog-friendly park is the perfect place for a Boxer to play, well away from traffic hazards, because Boxers can get so caught up in their games that they ignore everything else. Many Boxers also like to swim, but some don't. Let your Boxer be the guide. If she

In addition to walking your Boxer, give her at least two opportunities to run freely each day. Each of these exercise periods should last for 20 minutes or more.

loves water, you'll know it. If she doesn't, don't force her into the pool or lake.

The ways to exercise your adult Boxer are as varied as your imagination. Regular exercise will keep her younger longer and may even do the same for you!

ADVANCED TRAINING

A Boxer's native intelligence allows her to do many things, and Boxers often excel in competitive activities and noncompetitive service jobs.

CONFORMATION: Dog showing, or Conformation, is probably what most people think of when they think of dog competitions. Dog showing is truly a world unto itself, and for many people it becomes a full-time job. Basically, the competition works like this: Boxers are judged against other Boxers to find a Winner's Dog and a Winner's Bitch. These winning Boxers are then shown against what are called specials, the Boxers that have already won championships. When an overall winning dog is found from this group, it becomes the current Best of Breed (BOB).

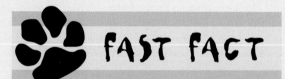

FAST FACT

Conformation is a very structured, formalized activity. If you choose to show your Boxer and act as her handler, study and practice the rules well ahead of time. Classes in show handling will hone your skills. Another option for your first show or two is to hire a professional handler to take your Boxer through her paces in the show ring. After observing this process, you can then take over.

Since Boxers are in the American Kennel Club's working dog group, this winning Boxer then competes against the winning dogs from other working dog breeds, such as Great Danes, Rottweilers, and Dobermans. The winner here challenges the winning dogs from the sporting, hound, terrier, toy, nonsporting, and herding groups to find the overall Best in Show. These competitions draw thousands of spectators; some, like the famous Westminster Kennel Club Dog Show, are broadcast on national television.

OBEDIENCE: Your Boxer doesn't have to be a beauty queen to become an Obedience champion, but she does have to have a good head on her shoulders. In Obedience competitions there are three main classes—the Regular class, the Open class, and the Utility class—and each is more difficult than the last. For example, in the regular class, a dog must get passing scores on these exercises: heeling on leash and figure-8, standing for examination, heeling free, recall, long sit, and long down.

To qualify in the Open class, a dog must do all of the above, plus drop on recall, retrieve on a flat surface, retrieve over a high jump, and successfully clear a broad jump.

PRIMPING FOR SHOW

If you plan to show your Boxer, you'll have to groom and primp her far more thoroughly than if she's just a companion animal. You'll need to trim her whiskers, ears, and any stray hairs. For shows, Boxers' muzzles are shined up with petroleum jelly and their white areas are chalked or powdered (like George Washington's wigs!). Most show dog owners and handlers prepare a show kit that has everything they will need for a contest: a cordless trimmer, white grooming chalk, a small soft brush for applying the chalk, Vaseline, Visine, a large soft grooming brush, show sheen, whitening shampoo, and a towel. A Boxer club or organization can show you how to groom a Boxer for competition.

Passing the Utility class is even more difficult. Here a dog must pass a signal exercise, several scent discriminations, a directed retrieve, and a directed jump.

If you're interested in Obedience competitions for your Boxer, it's wise to find a good training center as early as possible. For more information about either showing or Obedience, contact the American Kennel Club, or check the AKC's Web site, www.akc.org. If you live in Canada, the Canadian Kennel Club's Web site, www.ckc.ca, has information on shows and events. The same type of information is available to Boxer owners who live in Great Britain or Northern Ireland on the Kennel Club of the United Kingdom's Web site, www.thekennelclub.org.uk.

AGILITY: Agility competitions have recently exploded in popularity, mainly because they're great fun for both dogs and their handlers. They are patterned after horse jumping contests and involve obstacle courses that each dog must complete as quickly as possible, with a minimum of "faults." The dogs must jump over water, leap over hurdles, weave around poles, negotiate a teeter-totter, and navigate other such challenges. A fault is registered if the task isn't done perfectly. Needless to say, Boxers who excel at Agility competitions must be physically fit, self-confident, and smart. Again, the AKC, Canadian Kennel Club, or Kennel Club of the United Kingdom can steer you in the right direction if this sport interests you.

Because of their athletic nature, Boxers enjoy Agility competitions, which require dogs to successfully negotiate such obstacles as jumps and weave poles.

FLYBALL: Another competitive dog sport that's gaining in popularity is Flyball. It's great fun to watch. The competition consists of teams of four dogs and their handlers, and it's basically a relay race. The teams compete against each other, with the dogs running, leaping over hurdles, and springing open a box so a tennis ball pops out. The dog catches the ball and races back to her handler, with the fastest team winning. With their athleticism and sense of fun, Boxers are especially well suited to this new sport.

CANINE MUSICAL FREESTYLE AND HEELWORK TO MUSIC: Another opportunity for fun is Canine Musical Freestyle. This newer dog sport consists of music, tricks, Obedience, costumes, creativity, and a good dose of applause. Also known as "dog dancing," this sport requires a dog and her handler to execute tricks and Obedience maneuvers in a dance-type routine to music.

Heelwork to Music, a similar but less theatrical version of this sport, focuses more on Obedience skills. A dog and her handler are required to perform specific skills at each level of competition. The World Canine Freestyle Organization (WCFO) is the only organization that currently sanctions and titles dogs in Freestyle and Heelwork to Music competitions. More information can be found on this group's Web site, www.worldcaninefreestyle.org.

SERVICE WORK: Beyond participating in competitions, Boxers are also often employed in service to humankind. One of their most important roles is in pet therapy. Pet therapy? Yep, your dog acts as a therapist for you every day, but perhaps you already know that. If you've had a difficult day at work or at school, don't you instantly feel better when your Boxer greets you at the door, tail wagging, body all aquiver to see you? Dogs can provide this wonderful service for others, too—visiting and playing for a while with those suffering from pain in hospitals or loneliness in nursing homes. Therapy dogs visit care facilities regularly and become friends whom everyone looks forward to seeing.

THE COSTS OF COMPETITION

If you decide to get involved in competition sports with your Boxer, the annual cost of owning your dog will skyrocket, as you add on the following expenses:

Entry fees: $20 to $30 for each class entered. Depending on which sports and how many you compete in with your dog, entry fees for one show or trial can run from $20 to $100, or more.

Transportation: Fuel for your car or motor home to drive to shows within driving distance, and plane fare for important shows farther from home, such as the American Boxer Club's annual National Specialty show.

Lodging: Hotel or motel rooms range from $80 to several hundred dollars a night, depending on quality, location, and whether or not the pet fee charged by the hotel is refundable. At some events, participants are permitted to camp on the show grounds. If you own a motor home or camping trailer, this option usually costs from $15 to $50 a night.

Meals away from home: Budget appropriately, depending on your appetite and tastes.

Handler's fees: $100 to $600 or more per show. Hiring a professional handler to exhibit your Boxer in Conformation, instead of handling him yourself, can increase your dog's chances of success in the show ring, but the cost of earning those awards will increase as well.

Photographs of wins: When your Boxer wins at a show, captures a title, or earns a perfect score, you will want to get a photograph to remember the day. Sponsoring clubs arrange to have one or more professional photographers on site at the show to provide that service to exhibitors. Dog show photographers generally charge between $25 and $35 per print.

Therapy work, however, is not for every Boxer. A therapy dog must be very well-trained and even-tempered. She must enjoy crowds and meeting new people, and she can't get upset if a child pokes a finger in her ear. In fact, therapy dogs generally must have earned certification as a Canine Good Citizen (see page 30–33), as well as certification from an animal assisted-therapy association.

If you and your Boxer would enjoy doing this kind of fulfilling work, you can get all the information you need from the Delta Society or Therapy Dogs International, Inc. (see Organizations to Contact at the back of this book).

SEARCH AND RESCUE: Boxers are known for their extra-keen sense of smell, so they often work as search-and-rescue dogs, too. In this line of work, Boxers and their owners work together, tracking and trying to recover lost children, Alzheimer's patients who've wandered away, and, perhaps, dead bodies. This is a physically vigorous and mentally challenging job for both dog and master, but it, too, can be very rewarding work. The dog/human teams must be willing to go almost anywhere at a moment's notice, with search-and-rescue teams often traveling halfway around the world. SAR teams must also be able to function well in wilderness settings for several days at a time.

FAST FACT

Search-and-rescue teams (dog and human) must train together for hundreds of hours and be in superb physical shape.

For more information about search-and-rescue work for you and your Boxer, the best place to start is by contacting members of your local law enforcement agency. They'll be able to tell you what search-and-rescue organizations they work with.

❧❧❧❧

Always remember, no matter what activity you decide to share with your adult Boxer, you will undoubtedly find great joy and satisfaction in being a partner with your dog. She will surely feel the same way.

CHAPTER EIGHT

The Later Years and Saying Good-bye

Just like people, Boxers develop various ailments as they age. Unfortunately, Boxers can begin to age in what seems like the blink of an eye. By age seven, your Boxer will be considered a senior dog, but there are steps you can take to make her silver years as comfortable as possible. Simply pay attention to the physical changes she's undergoing, and deal with them as they arise. This can make your Boxer's later

As your Boxer ages, it is normal for her to have less energy.

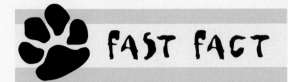

FAST FACT

Some elderly Boxers will suffer from old-dog syndrome, also known as cognitive dysfunction syndrome. This is the canine equivalent of senility.

years as fulfilling as every other period of her life.

Like you, your Boxer will be prone to arthritis as she ages. And like you, too, she may benefit from over-the-counter remedies such as a glucosamine/chondroitin formulation that works as a joint lubricant. Ask your vet if this type of treatment is right for your Boxer.

Boxers seem especially prone to another ailment of aging—corneal ulcers. These are ulcers that appear on the surface of the dog's eye and can cause blindness if not treated promptly. Remember to check your Boxer's eyes thoroughly every few weeks, especially as she ages.

When you're brushing or bathing your elder Boxer, run your hands over her body to make sure she's not developing any lumps or bumps. Unfortunately, the senior years are the time when most cancers develop in dogs. Report any suspicious growths to your veterinarian as soon as possible.

Remember, too, to check your Boxer's teeth and gums. As she ages, gingival hyperplasia may appear. This disease causes the gums to grow over the teeth and can be quite unpleasant for your dog. You can avoid it with regular tooth brushing.

Another symptom of aging in some Boxers is incontinence. Try not to let your canine pal's sudden puddles around the house upset you, because she'll already be upset

At about seven years of age, a Boxer's muzzle will begin to turn silver or white. Thus the expression *silver years*.

enough for both of you. Just give her additional opportunities each day to relieve herself outdoors (almost as if she were a puppy again), and her accidents can be kept to a minimum.

When your Boxer reaches her silver years, your veterinarian will likely recommend periodic blood work for her and extra exams. These procedures can help detect any developing kidney or liver problems, heart disease, adrenal disorders, or cancer. All are common problems in aging dogs. As in humans, if these problems are caught early, treatment is easier and the prognosis is better.

NUTRITION

If you've kept your Boxer fit and trim in her younger years, she should move into her senior years without gaining too much extra weight. Keeping strict control of your dog's food intake is not always easy, however. Dogs have a knack for finding food, and if they find it, they eat it.

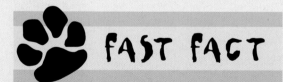

FAST FACT

It's best not to introduce a new puppy into a home with an elderly Boxer. As the new dog matures, she may become aggressive and try to dominate the weaker, older dog.

That includes food off kids' plates and out of the cat's bowl, not to mention the treats and snacks family members might slip her. So if you find that your Boxer has become a heavy geriatric, you need to get the excess weight off her for her own health and comfort. Excess weight, especially in the senior years, puts additional stress on vital organs and joints, shortening your dog's life.

It may be as simple as just giving your dog less food now that she's older. Also, there are quality senior dog foods on the market that are lower in fat. If she'll eat raw vegetables, they will provide bulk and nutrition, making your dog feel full, without being full of calories.

As dogs age, their metabolism changes and they don't absorb vitamins and minerals from food as well as they once did. Many older Boxers, therefore, benefit from supplements. Some Boxer owners find that extra vitamins C and E, along with calcium, essential fatty acids like fish oil, and even a kelp or seaweed formula can increase their pets' vitality in old age. Check with your vet or research pet supplements for aging dogs to see what might be helpful for your Boxer.

EXERCISE

Even though your dog is older, she still needs, and likely wants, regular

Although she may be slowing down physically, your senior Boxer still needs daily exercise to keep her fit and trim.

FAST FACT

Even if your older Boxer no longer seems eager to accompany you on walks, she'll likely be very disappointed if you stop taking her. So keep up a regular exercise regimen.

exercise. Exercise will help to prevent her from gaining weight and will keep her engaged in life. Even though she may not be as frisky as she once was, she's still curious about what's going on in the neighborhood. So daily walks, at a pace your older Boxer can manage, will be a pleasure you both can still savor. Keep an eye on her stamina, though, and head for home when it appears that she's getting fatigued.

If your Boxer enjoyed swimming when she was younger, she'll probably still like to swim, and no other exercise is better for her arthritic joints. Again, keep an eye on her stamina, and don't leave her alone in the water. At an advanced age, a dog may have a hard time climbing out of a pool or lake that was once no problem for her to negotiate at all.

Old age is, however, the time to eliminate strenuous running and jumping games with your dog. Running and leaping for a Frisbee, for example, can put an unnecessary strain on her heart and her joints. Stick with walks and swims when it's not too hot or too cold outside.

SAYING GOOD-BYE

Eventually, inevitably, you and your dear friend will have to part. What can be even more difficult, emotionally, is that you'll have to decide when it's time for your loyal companion to die. Unless your Boxer dies peacefully and suddenly at home, it is very likely that she'll have to be euthanatized to spare her the pain and suffering of dying slowly

EASING YOUR BOXER'S PASSING

Euthanasia is a Greek word that means, roughly, "good death." Now it refers mainly to a painless death, but it can still be a "good death" for your Boxer if she's with the people she loves and trusts at the end. Then she'll be peaceful and even happy as she passes.

sleep, and for love. If she had a say in the matter, she would surely trust you to decide her end. Trust yourself. You'll know when disease or injury is robbing your friend of her enjoyment of life and of your company. If no recovery is possible, it's time. If she can no longer move around without great pain, or if she's no longer eating, it's time. If you want, spend a final weekend with her, so the family can share time with her, love her, and say good-bye.

The final trip to the vet's will be very emotional, but try to stay composed for your dog's sake. She doesn't want to see you upset. The actual process of euthanasia is painless for the dog. The vet will usually administer a sedative first, so your proud friend will fall asleep. Then an overdose of anesthesia is administered, and the dog's heart simply stops beating.

It's perfectly natural to grieve after such an event. Let your grief run its course. Once you've come to terms with your loss, and you feel that you are ready, perhaps you'll want to start looking for a new Boxer puppy.

Photos of you and your Boxer in happier times may help to ease the grieving process.

from disease. As difficult as this decision is, you owe it to her.

It might help to think of it this way. Your Boxer has trusted you for everything all her life—for nourishment, for fun, for a warm place to

Organizations to Contact

**American Animal
Hospital Association**
12575 West Bayaud Ave.
Lakewood, CO 80228
Phone: 303-986-2800
Fax: 800-252-2242
Email: info@aahanet.org
Web site: www.aahanet.org

American Boxer Club
Sandy Orr, corresponding secretary
7106 N. 57th St.
Omaha, NE 68152
Phone: 509-747-3254
Fax: 509-747-1406
Email: abcsecretary@cox.net
Web site: www.americanboxerclub.org

American Kennel Club
260 Madison Ave
New York, NY 10016
Phone: 212-696-8200
Web site: www.akc.org

American Veterinary Medical Assn.
1931 N. Meacham Road, Suite 100
Schaumburg, IL 60173-4360
Phone: 847-925-8070
Fax: 847-925-1329
Email: avmainfo@avma.org
Web site: www.avma.org

Anglian Boxer Club (U.K.)
Dave Rushton, Secretary
Old Free School, More Hall Lane
Bolsterstone, Sheffield S36 3ST
United Kingdom
Phone: 0114 2881079
Fax: 01698 827486
Email: dave@davnetteboxers.co.uk
Web site: www.anglianboxerclub.co.uk

Association of Pet Dog Trainers
150 Executive Center Drive, Box 35
Greenville, SC 29615
Phone: 800-738-3647
Fax: 864-331-0767
Email: information@apdt.com
Web site: www.apdt.com

Boxer Breed Club of Canada
Sharon Simpson
2539 Princess Ave.
Brandon, MB R7B 0J5
Canada
Phone: 205-727-1429
Fax: 204-728-9288
Email: everlongboxers@hotmail.com
Web site: www.boxerbreedclub
    ofcanada.com

Boxer Rescue Foundation
P.O. Box 57106
Phoenix, AZ 85079
Web site: www.boxerrescue
     foundation.com
Email: weluvmail@boxerrescue
     foundation.com

The Canadian Kennel Club
89 Skyway Avenue, Suite 100
Etobicoke, Ontario
M9W 6R4
Canada
Phone: 416-675-5511
Fax: 416-675-6506
Email: information@ckc.ca
Web site: www.ckc.ca/en

**Canine Eye Registration
Foundation**
1717 Philo Road
P.O. Box 3007
Urbana, IL 61803-3007
Phone: 217-693-4800
Fax: 217-693-4801
Email: cerf@vmdb.org
Web site: www.vmdb.org/cerf.html

Delta Society
875 124th Avenue NE, Suite 101
Bellevue, WA 98005
Phone: 425-226-7357
Fax: 425-679-5539
Email: info@deltasociety.org
Web site: www.deltasociety.org

**The Kennel Club
of the United Kingdom**
1-5 Clarges Street
Piccadilly, London W1J 8AB
United Kingdom
Phone: 0870 606 6750
Fax: 020 7518 1058
Web site: www.thekennelclub.org.uk

**National Association of Dog
Obedience Instructors**
PMB 369
729 Grapevine Hwy
Hurst, TX 76054-2085
Email: corrsec2@nadoi.org
Web site: www.nadoi.org

**National Association of
Professional Pet Sitters**
17000 Commerce Parkway, Suite C
Mt. Laurel, NJ 08054
Phone: 856-439-0324
Fax: 856-439-0525
Email: napps@ahint.com
Web site: www.petsitters.org

**North American Dog Agility
Council (NADAC)**
11522 South Highway 3
Cataldo, ID 83810
Email: info@nadac.com
Web site: www.nadac.com

North American Flyball Association (NAFA)
1400 West Devon Avenue, #512
Chicago, IL 60660
Phone: 800-318-6312
Fax: same as phone
Email: flyball@flyball.org
Web site: www.flyball.org

Pet Sitters International
418 East King Street
King, NC 27021-9163
Phone: 336-983-9222
Fax: 336-983-3755
Web site: www.petsit.com

Therapy Dogs International, Inc.
88 Bartley Road
Flanders, NJ 07836
Phone: 973-252-9800
Fax: 973-252-7171
Email: tdi@gti.net
Web site: www.tdi-dog.org

United States Dog Agility Association, Inc. (USDAA)
P.O. Box 850955
Richardson, TX 75085-0955
Phone: 972-487-2200
Fax: 972-272-4404
Email: info@usdaa.com
Web site: www.usdaa.com

World Canine Freestyle Organization (WCFO)
P.O. Box 350122
Brooklyn, NY 11235-2525
Phone: 718-332-8336
Fax: 718-646-2686
Email: wcfodogs@aol.com
Web site: www.worldcanine
     freestyle.org

UK National Pet Register
74 North Albert Street, Dept 2
Fleetwood, Lancashire
FY7 6BJ
United Kingdom
Web site: www.nationalpetregister.org

Further Reading

Arden, Andrea. *Dog-Friendly Dog Training*. Hoboken, N.J.: Howell Book House, 2007.

Beauchamp, Richard. *Boxers for Dummies*. New York: Hungry Minds, 2000.

Eldredge, Debra M. et al. *Dog Owner's Home Veterinary Handbook*. Hoboken, N.J.: Howell Book House, 2007.

Gallagher, Cynthia P. *Boxers*. Neptune City, N.J.: TFH Publications, 2006.

Hoffman, Matthew. *Dogs: The Ultimate Care Guide: Good Health, Loving Care, Maximum Longevity*. Emmaus, Pa.: Rodale Books, 2000.

Kilcommons, Brian. *Good Owners, Great Dogs*. New York: Grand Central Publishing, 1999.

Spitzer, Karla. *The Everything Boxer Book*. Avon, Mass.: Adams Media, 2006.

Walker, Joan Hustace. *The Boxer Handbook*. Hauppauge, N.Y.: Barron's Educational Series, 2000.

Internet Resources

www.americanboxerclub.org

Everything you want to know about Boxers, including a history of the breed, local Boxer clubs, show information, and health topics.

www.akc.org/breeds/boxer/index.cfm

This page contains the American Kennel Club's description of the Boxer breed standard.

www.aspca.org/apcc

The ASPCA Animal Poison Control Center provides lifesaving information for pet owners. The center also has a hot line available for emergencies: 888-426-4435

http://boxerclubofcanada.com

A Canadian site with information about shows, competitive activities, and service opportunities for your Boxer.

www.boxerworld.com

This site claims to be the ultimate resource for all things Boxer-related. International in scope, it's lighthearted and entertaining.

www.boxerdogplanet.com

A forum where Boxer owners can communicate with each other.

www.ckc.ca/en/Default.aspx?tabid=99&BreedCode=BXR

This page contains the Canadian Kennel Club's description of the Boxer breed standard.

www.canismajor.com/dog

This Web site has a tremendous library of articles about dogs, covering everything from hereditary health issues to breed profiles. Have a question about dogs? You can look it up here.

www.thekennelclub.org.uk/item/45

This page contains the Kennel Club of the United Kingdom's description of the Boxer breed standard.

www.petfinder.com

A nationwide database of adoptable pets, which also provides listings of shelters and Boxer rescue groups.

www.petrix.com/dognames

Can't think of a catchy name for your Boxer? This Web site will give you all kinds of ideas, from traditional to strangely unique!

www.petsitters.org

The Web site of the National Association of Professional Pet Sitters can be used to help Boxer owners locate a professional pet sitter in their area.

www.thepetcenter.com

Calling itself the Internet Animal Hospital, this site offers articles and information on dog health care and diseases.

Index

adenovirus, 54, 55, 73
Agility competitions, 31, 39, 91–93
    See also dog shows
American Animal Hospital Association
    (AAHA), 44–45
American Boarding Kennel Association
    (ABKA), 81
American Boxer Club, 10, 21
American Boxer Rescue Association, 36
American Kennel Club (AKC), 10, 14,
    20–21, 40, 90–91
    and the Canine Good Citizen (CGC)
        test, 30–33, 94
aortic stenosis, 85
arthritis, 97
Association of American Feed Control
    Officials (AAFCO), 59
Assyrians, 17
    See also breed history

baby gates, 51
Bang Away (champion Boxer), 21
barking, 24, 30
bathing, 64–65
    See also grooming
bite and jaw structure, 12
    See also physical characteristics
biting, 25, 30, 31, 46
bloat and torsion, 85–86
boarding kennels, 80–81
    See also traveling
bordetella, 54, 71, 73
The Boxer Review, 42
Boxers
    breed history, 17–23
    breed standards, 10–14, 19, 23
    choosing of, as pets, 35–44
    curiosity of, 9–10, 45

and gas, 16
gender differences, 35–36
and health issues, 40, 43, 54–57, 61, 71,
    74, 82–88, 97–100
intelligence of, 9–10, 45, 89–90
and jobs, 10, 14–15, 19, 23, 90, 93–95
naming of, 18
number registered, 23
and personality, 14–16, 28, 36, 43
physical characteristics, 9, 10–14, 22,
    23, 71, 82
popularity of, 9, 21
as senior dogs, 96–100
size, 11, 71
and socialization, 31, 60–62, 74–76
and vaccinations, 25, 54–55, 71, 73
    See also ownership, dog; puppies
Brabanter Bullenbeiser, 18
    See also breed history
breed history, 17–23
breed standards, 10–14, 19, 23
breeders, 10, 21, 39–42, 43, 83
brindle. *See* colors
brushing, 63–64
    See also grooming
Bullenbeisers (mastiff), 17–18
    See also breed history

Canada, 10, 20, 21, 23
Canadian Kennel Club, 91
Canadian Veterinary Medical Association
    (CVMA), 59
cancer, 84, 97
Canine Eye Registration Foundation
    (CERF), 40
Canine Good Citizen (CGC) test, 30–33, 94
Canine IQ Test, 38
Canine Musical Freestyle, 93

cardiomyopathy, 43, 84–85
CH Roll von Vogelsberg (Boxer), 19
chewing, 38
coat, 13, 82
    See also physical characteristics
cognitive dysfunction syndrome, 97
collars, 47–49
colors, 9, 13
    See also physical characteristics
commands, 32–33, 37, 60, 76–78
    See also training
Conformation dog shows, 10–11, 13, 14,
    21, 90
    See also dog shows
contract, puppy sale, 41
    See also breeders
Coren, Stanley, 38
corneal ulcers, 97
coronavirus, 54, 55, 71, 73
costs, 29, 47, 94
crates, 49–51, 67, 80
curiosity, 9–10, 45

Dampf von Dom (Boxer), 20
Dawson, Allon, 23
death, 100–101
Delta Society, 95
dental care, 66, 83, 97
diseases. See health issues
distemper, 54, 55, 71, 73
dog shows, 10–11, 13, 14, 21, 31, 41, 43,
    90–94

ears, 13, 14–15, 21, 64–65, 82
euthanasia, 100–101
exercise, 15, 30, 73, 89, 98–100
eyes, 12, 83
    and disease, 43, 97

fear-imprint period, 61–62
    See also socialization
fencing, 28
first aid, 53
flash, 13

See also colors
fleas, 56, 71–72
    See also parasites
Flocki (first Boxer), 18
Flyball competitions, 39, 93
    See also dog shows
flying, 79–80
    See also traveling
food, 43, 58–60, 74, 84, 88–89, 98

gas, 16
gender, 35–36
Germany, 18–19, 23
Good Citizen Dog Scheme, 31
grooming, 32, 63–66, 91
guide dogs, 10

Harris, R. C. and Phoebe, 21
head and muzzle, 11–12
    See also physical characteristics
health issues, 40, 71, 82–88
    and hereditary disorders, 40, 43, 55, 74,
        84–85
    and parasites, 54, 56–57, 61
    and senior dogs, 97–100
    and vaccinations, 25, 54–55, 71, 73
    See also Boxers
heart disease, 84–85
heartworms, 56–57
heatstroke, 86–88
Heelwork to Music, 93
    See also dog shows
hepatitis, 71
hereditary disorders, 40, 43, 55, 74, 84–85
    See also health issues
hip dysplasia, 40, 43, 55, 74
home puppy-proofing, 45–46
    See also ownership, dog
housetraining, 37, 50, 66–68
    See also training

identification, 24, 25–26
    See also ownership, dog
incontinence, 97–98

insurance, pet, 29
intelligence, 9–10, 45, 89–90
The Intelligence of Dogs (Coren), 38

jobs (for Boxers), 10, 14–15, 19, 23, 90, 93–95
Johanson, Jake, 62

Kennel Club of the United Kingdom, 31, 91

leashes, 49
legal issues, 29–30
　See also ownership, dog
Lehman, Herbert H., 20
leptospirosis, 54, 55, 71, 73
licensing, 26
　See also ownership, dog
Lyme disease, 54, 71, 72, 73

manners, 68–69
　See also training
microchips, 25–26
　See also identification
microfilaria (heartworm), 56–57
minerals and vitamins, 58, 59, 98
　See also food
mosquitoes, 56
My Life with Boxers (Stockmann), 19

nail care, 65–66, 83
　See also grooming
neutering, 26–29, 36
Northern Boxer Club, 23
nutrition. *See* food

Obedience competitions, 31, 90–91
　See also dog shows
Obedience Personality Test, 38
obesity, 84
ownership, dog, 24–25, 30–31
　choosing your Boxer, 35–44
　costs of, 29, 47, 94
　identification, 24, 25–26

legal issues, 29–30
licensing, 26
and pet insurance, 29
preparing for, 34–35, 45–47, 51
spaying or neutering, 26–29, 36
and supplies, 47–51
See also Boxers

parainfluenza, 54, 55, 71, 73
parasites, 54, 56–57, 61, 71–73
　See also health issues
parvovirus, 54, 55, 71, 73
pedigree, 41
　See also breeders
personality, 14–16, 28, 36, 43
pet insurance, 29
pet sitters, 81
physical characteristics, 9, 10–14, 22, 23, 71, 82
popularity, 9, 21
potty training. *See* housetraining
proportion, 11
　See also physical characteristics
puppies
　aptitude testing, 38
　caring for, 52–55, 58–60, 63–66
　choosing, 36–39, 42–44
　training, 60–63, 66–69
　vaccination schedule, 54–55
　See also Boxers
Puppy Aptitude Test, 38
push-ups, 78
　See also training

rabies, 25, 26, 54, 55, 71, 73
registration papers, 41
　See also breeders
rescue organizations, 36, 39, 40

search and rescue, 10, 95
senior dogs, 96–100
　See also Boxers
separation anxiety, 62–63
Sirrah Crest Kennels, 21

size, 11, 71
    See also physical characteristics
socialization, 31, 60–62, 74–76
spaying, 26–29, 36
Standard of Perfection, 10, 39
    See also breed standards
Stockmann, Friederun, 19–20, 21, 23
Stockmann, Phillip, 19
studbook, 18, 19
supplies, 47–51
    first aid, 53

tail, 13–14
tattoos, 25, 26
    See also identification
temperament. *See* personality
therapy dogs, 10, 93–95
Therapy Dogs International, Inc., 95
ticks, 56, 72–73
    See also parasites
Tom (bulldog), 18
toys, 38, 51
training, 33, 36–37, 60–63, 68–69, 76–78
    advanced, 89–95

house (potty), 37, 50, 66–68
    obedience, 15
traveling, 78–80

United Kingdom, 10, 21, 23
United States, 20–21, 23
United States Boxer Association (USBA),
    41

vaccinations, 25, 54–55, 71, 73
    See also health issues
veterinarians, 54–56, 80–81, 101
    choosing, 44–45
    See also health issues
vitamins and minerals, 58, 59, 98
    See also food
Volhard, Jack and Wendy, 38
Von Dom Kennels, 19–20

Westminster Kennel Club Show, 20, 21, 90
World Canine Freestyle Organization
    (WCFO), 93
World War I, 19
World War II, 21

Contributors

CHAD HAUTMANN is a novelist and freelance writer. His first novel, *Billie's Ghost*, was published by Penguin in 2004. An award-winning environmental writer, Chad has published articles, stories, and poems in magazines around the country. He is a lifelong dog (and cat) owner and lives in Naples, Florida, with his wife and two children. His second novel, *Magic and Grace*, is slated to appear in the spring of 2008.

Senior Consulting Editor **GARY KORSGAARD, DVM,** has had a long and distinguished career in veterinary medicine. After graduating from The Ohio State University's College of Veterinary Medicine in 1963, he spent two years as a captain in the Veterinary Corps of the U.S. Army. During that time he attended the Walter Reed Army Institute of Research and became Chief of the Veterinary Division for the Sixth Army Medical Laboratory at the Presidio, San Francisco.

In 1968 Dr. Korsgaard founded the Monte Vista Veterinary Hospital in Concord, California, where he practiced for 32 years as a small animal veterinarian. He is a past president of the Contra Costa Veterinary Association, and was one of the founding members of the Contra Costa Veterinary Emergency Clinic, serving as president and board member of that hospital for nearly 30 years.

Dr. Korsgaard retired in 2000, and currently enjoys golf, hiking, international travel, and spending time with his wife Susan and their three children and four grandchildren.